ALBERT BRETON is a member of the Department of Political Economy at the University of Toronto.
ANTHONY SCOTT is a member of the Department of Economics at the University of British Columbia.

This book provides a new way of looking at the old problem of the assignment of powers in federal structures. A federal state is, by definition, one in which there exists two or more jurisdictional levels between which authority over domains of public policies has to be assigned. In Canada, for example, the provinces have been given exclusive jurisdiction over education; currency and international trade are assigned to the federal government; and both levels have concurrent authority in agriculture. Furthermore, in Canada, as in all federal states, the assignment of powers changes over time in an almost continuous way.

The theory developed in this book suggests that the total amount of resources – defined in the broadest possible way – used up in running the public sector varies with the way powers are assigned to different jurisdictional levels; or, to put it differently, varies with the degree of centralization in the public sector. The absorption of resources for the purpose of running the public sector – to be distinguished from resources absorbed in the supply of the public policies themselves – takes four forms; resources used up by citizens to signal their preferences to governments, or to move from one jurisdiction to another; and those used up by governments to administer themselves, and to co-ordinate their activities.

Two basic models are examined. In one, the assignment of powers which uses up the smallest amount of resources is analysed. In the other the assignment which is produced by politicians and bureaucrats operating within the framework of representative governments is studied. The two models are applied to the particular problems posed by redistribution and stabilization powers. A new approach to inter-jurisdictional grants derived from the basic theory is also suggested.

ALBERT BRETON

ANTHONY SCOTT

The economic constitution of federal states

UNIVERSITY OF TORONTO PRESS
Toronto Buffalo London

© University of Toronto Press 1978
Toronto Buffalo London
Printed in Canada

Library of Congress in Publication Data

Breton, Albert.
  The economic constitution of federal states.

  Includes bibliographical references and index.
  1. Federal government. 2. Economic policy. I. Scott, Anthony, joint author.
  II. Title.
  JC355.B77   320'.2   77-18526
  ISBN 0-8020-5410-2

We dedicate this book
to the memory of FERNAND CADIEUX
and to HENRY ANGUS
remembering their friendship
and intellectual influence

Acknowledgments

A considerable amount of our research time over the last four years has been devoted to the preparation of this book. The successive drafts – four in all – as well as papers and seminars based on them, which we have delivered during these years, attest to the unmistakable fact that there is but limited resemblance between what we are now presenting to the public and what we started out doing.

The evolution of our ideas was governed partly by the dynamics of our approach to federalism, which was itself conditioned by our desire to produce a unified framework to analyse the layered structure of government, but it was also determined in no small measure by the discussions and the written or verbal comments and criticisms which we have received, together or separately, from numerous friends and colleagues.

We cannot hope to name them all. However, beyond a blanket 'thank you' to all who have helped us, we would like to thank in a special way all those who, at one time or another, have provided us with detailed comments, generally in written form, which have had a profound influence on our work. They include Thomas Borcherding, James Buchanan, Jesse Burkhead, John Graham, Harry Johnson, Julie Margolis, James Maxwell, Peter Mieszkowski, Wallace Oates, Alan Peacock, Mark Sproule-Jones, Gordon Tullock, Richard Wagner, and John Weymark.

In addition, we would like to thank G.C. Archibald, H.F. Angus, Peter Bohn, Thomas Courchene, John Dales, David Donaldson, Francesco Forte, Douglas Hartle, John Hartwick, Harold Hochman, David Mayston, Melville McMillan, Gilles Paquet, Antonio Pedone, Jim Taylor, and Jim Wilen, who, in private conversations or as discussants of papers given by either one of us have helped us to see the problem of federalism and those of modelling it differently and have helped us with some of our difficulties.

Given the length of the above list and the diversity of approaches and opinions which it necessarily entails, it is superfluous to insist that every one of them should be considered innocent of what we have perpetrated, though we know that not to be the whole truth.

We must also thank in a special way Shanon Grauer and Kathy White who, at different times, have served as diligent research assistants, and Jessie Leger and Martin Samuels, who have typed and retyped the various drafts of the manuscript.

Finally, we wish to express our sincere gratitude to the Canada Council, which, through its Killam Awards Program, has made it possible for both of us to be relieved, for a total of one year, from the duties and drudgeries that afflict academics in the usual course of affairs. Without that help we would not have been able to meet and work together and thus the present book would not have been written. It has been published with the help of grants from the Social Science Federation of Canada, using funds provided by the Canada Council, from the Publications Fund of the University of Toronto Press, and from the University of Toronto.

AB / AS

Contents

PART ONE
CONCEPTS

1

Introduction and background

The main task we have set for ourselves in this book is that of formulating models that would allow us to understand the nature and the working of the forces that govern the assignment of functions or powers to the various jurisdictional levels that make up federal states. We wish, in other words, to be able to explain why it is that the governments located at one particular jurisdictional level – the provincial level or the local level, for example – have the authority to make laws, to regulate, or to spend money on certain activities and not on others. Why, for example, have provincial governments in Canada been assigned powers with respect to education and to agricultural marketing boards and not with respect to weights and measures and to banking?

Because we seek to provide answers to questions of this kind that are general enough to apply in principle to all cases, and which go beyond the imprints of politicians and of constitutional lawyers, we have chosen 'The Economic Constitution of Federal States' as the title of our study. This should underline the distinction between our work and one which would focus on the political or legal constitution of federations as well as emphasize that our approach and methods of analysis are essentially economic.

An earlier mimeographed draft of this study was circulated under the title of 'A Theory of the Structure of the Public Sector.' In choosing such a title we had sought to avoid the use of the word federalism, simply because the subject matter of our research, though relevant to federal states, did extend beyond governmental structures that are constitutionally recognized as federal structures. We abandoned that title for reasons of euphony. We wish to emphasize, our change of mind on title notwithstanding, that there exists a basic non-correspondence between what is generally meant by the word federalism and the reality analysed in this book.

This non-correspondence arises from the fact that municipal, local, and other junior governments play an essential role in our analysis and in most other economic models, but their presence in a given public sector does not of itself make it a federal state. For example, France and the United Kingdom are constituted of *préfectures* or *départements* and of local authorities, but they are not in any way federal states. However, our analysis applies to these two countries just as it applies to Australia, Canada, and the United States, which are officially known as federations.

The reader should therefore keep in mind that throughout this study we have used interchangeably words like federal structure, federal state, public sector structure, and federation to refer to the same reality, a reality which is broader than that usually covered by the word federalism.

2 PRIOR EXPLANATIONS

To analyse assignments in federal states, it is important to distinguish between initial assignments, which are invariably associated with the formation of federations, and reassignments. The former are more difficult to model for a number of reasons. There is first the fact of the small number of cases following upon the relatively rare event of the formation of new federations and of new states. There is also the fact that the differences associated with new federations and states appear to exceed the similarities, so that the student of this question is at a loss in seeking which variable or issue to emphasize.

The models we analyse in this book deal with problems of reassignment of powers and shed only very indirect light on the question of the origin of states in general and of federal states in particular. However, because initial conditions often have an important influence on later reassignments, we will digress briefly to examine some of the factors associated with initial conditions that have retained the attention of scholars of federalism. We do this for the reason just indicated, but also to stress why we have not pursued the line of analysis associated with these factors.

There are essentially three alternative, and possibly complementary, explanations for the origin of federal states in the economic and public finance literature broadly defined. One of these seeks a rationale for a public sector structure in cultural, linguistic, racial, religious, and / or other diversities of that nature. This rationale is essentially *ad hoc* and *ex post*, because even if it can tell us why some decentralized structures exist, it is of no use in explaining why other societies which are characterized by diverse cultures, languages, races, etc. are not structured on the basis of these diversities, or in understanding why decentralized structures exist in societies that are culturally, linguistically, racially, etc. homogeneous.

It is true, of course, and a matter of historical record, that some societies have been organized on a decentralized basis in an effort to cope with one diversity or another of the kind listed above, so that one does not want to dismiss this explanation out of hand. Once we have outlined the workings of our model later in this chapter, we will indicate to the reader how cultural, religious, linguistic, etc. diversity can be made to enter our model and how it can affect its operations. It is sufficient to note here that, of itself, diversity cannot serve as a basis on which to erect a theory of federalism.

The second rationale for a federal structure is the conjecture or assumption that lower-level or junior governments are more responsive to the preferences of citizens than are higher-level or senior ones. The best way to understand its meaning is to inquire into the frame of mind that is required for its birth. Imagine someone who has been brought up to think of the public sector as constituted of one government, a frame of mind often found in those whose views have been formed in the English or French classical political science tradition and certainly one that completely permeates all the literature of economics. If that person turned his or her attention to real world public sectors for a moment and observed a full hierarchy of government levels, he or she might be tempted, upon asking why all these jurisdictional levels exist, to answer that the lower levels, because they deal with fewer citizens, possibly with more homogeneous groups of preferences, and with local issues, are more responsive to the desires and demands of the local citizenry. That argument, because it has an air of plausibility about it, could then be used, as it has, to rationalize the existence of the whole set-up.[1]

The role of the assumption for that person serves in other words to explain why not all public policies are supplied by one unique super-government, a situation that is implicitly taken to characterize the 'normal' or 'natural' state of the world. To put it still differently, for someone in the classical frame of mind, if all levels of government could be taken to be equally responsive to the preferences of each citizen, there would exist only one government in the public sector.

If one is in a different frame of mind, namely, in one which assumes that governments are institutions that people create themselves for the purpose of resolving essentially collective issues, then it becomes impossible to understand how the public sector could be made up of only one government. The natural state of the world is one in which public sectors are characterized by a structure of jurisdictional levels. The assumption that junior governments are more responsive than senior governments is not necessary in such a framework.

1 This is effectively the view taken by one of us in earlier efforts to understand the nature of federalism. See A. Breton, 'Public Goods (and Federalism): A Reply,' *Canadian Journal of Economics and Political Science* XXXII 2 (May 1966) 241-2.

In other words, if governments exist to provide public policies that would not be provided otherwise, the search should not be for an assumption, building block, or factor that will help one to understand why a hierarchy of governments exist, but for a factor or assumption that will limit the number of levels and the number of governments. Consequently, in the remainder of this book, we assume that *ceteris paribus* all governments are equally responsive to the preferences of citizens and seek to explain the existence of a decentralized public sector structure in a different way.[2]

The third explanation for the existence of a public sector structure that one finds in the literature, and in particular in the literature of economics, is based on the notion that the policies supplied by governments are like public or non-private goods, or are characterized by externalities and / or economies of scale in consumption and in production. The decentralized structure of the public sector is then thought to be the product of balancing the benefits of centralization made possible by an exploitation of economies of scale against the cost of centralization resulting from the consumption of public-good-like policies by citizens in amounts or qualities which differ from those that are desired – a difference that is assumed to depend on the degree of dispersion of the distribution of citizens' preferences, which in turn is assumed to vary directly with the size of jurisdictions.

We devote Chapter 4 to a discussion and criticism of this approach and consequently need not dwell on it here. Suffice it to indicate that even though we do borrow from the work based on this approach, our reason for not adopting it is essentially that once it is recognized that production of public policies need not be carried on at the level at which decisions about consumption are made, the balancing described above collapses and the search must start anew for a factor or hypothesis that will set a limit to the number of governments and to the number of jurisdictional levels that constitute the public sector.

The discovery that the balancing of the costs and benefits of centralization cannot provide a rationale for a public sector structure is fairly new. Indeed, Tullock, who was among the first to diagnose the failure of this approach, also suggested that the cost of setting up governmental structures and the cost of operat-

2 It is possible, of course, that governments catering to populations made up of citizens who have the same preference patterns will appear to be more responsive than governments catering to populations in which the dispersion of tastes is large. Such appearances do not, however, necessarily imply differences in responsiveness, but are the outcome of the ease or cost of responding. For example, even if we assume that a local alderman and a federal MP are equally responsive, the former has the possibility of listening to every one of his constituents, while the latter certainly has not. The higher cost of responding facing the MP will play an important role in the remainder of this book.

ing them could serve as the needed limiting factor.[3] We took our cue from him, but carried his reasoning further, along the line of the modern work on transaction costs,[4] work which is providing a basis for an understanding of the existence and working of institutions.

3 A 'NEW' APPROACH

As just indicated, the approach to the operation of federal states which we are suggesting in this book rests on the presence of certain resource-using organizational activities. We did not wish to use the term transaction costs to describe these costs because we believed that these words are best reserved for the costs of buying and of selling private goods and services in ordinary markets. We decided to call them organizational costs because we believe that this expression well describes the use of resources in activities aimed at organizing the institutions needed for the provision of public policies.

As indicated in the last section, one of the organizational costs relevant for our analysis is administration costs. Following Tullock, we define these to be the costs of setting up governmental institutions and of running them. We distinguish, however, between the administration costs that pertain to activities that are internal to governments and those costs that apply to the task of co-ordinating activities between governments, and we call the second co-ordination costs. Consequently, on the supply side of the public sector, we have two kinds of organizational costs: internal administration costs or simply administration costs and external administration or co-ordination costs.

We could not stop with the supply side of the public sector and consequently extended the notion of resource-using organizational activities to the demand side. Our approach consists in postulating that citizens will use up resources for the purpose of obtaining bundles of public policies that correspond more exactly to the bundles they desire. We lump all the activities in which citizens engage for that purpose into two classes and call them signalling and mobility. On the demand side of the public sector, we then also have two kinds of organizational costs: signalling and mobility costs.

We devote space below[5] to a discussion of these four classes of costs and

3 G. Tullock, 'Federalism: Problems of Scale,' *Public Choice* VI (Spring 1969) 19-30
4 The classic reference is R.H. Coase, 'The Nature of the Firm,' in American Economic Association, *Readings in Price Theory* (Homewood: Richard D. Irwin, Inc. 1952) 331-51. See also the *Report on Maritime Union*, commissioned by the governments of Nova Scotia, New Brunswick, and Prince Edward Island (Fredericton: Queen's Printer 1970), and supporting studies.
5 Chapter 3, pp. 31ff.

examine their various components in some detail. We must, however, emphasize now that governments on the one hand and citizens on the other incur these costs because of the presence of economies of scale in production, procurement, and / or distribution and because many public policies possess the characteristics of public and non-private goods and display external economies and diseconomies. To illustrate, assume that there are economies of scale in the provision of sewage services. To insure that these economies are as fully exploited as possible, governments may find it advantageous to negotiate with each other and to co-ordinate their activities. The economies of scale may, in other words, induce governments to incur co-ordination costs. The general idea that the use of resources on administration and co-ordination by governments and on signalling and mobility by citizens rests on the presence of economies of scale, on the publicness of certain goods and services, on externalities, or on all of these provides a bridge between the models to be developed in forthcoming chapters and the older – and, as we hope to show in Chapter 4, less satisfactory – approach to federalism.

We refer to economies of scale and to externalities related to goods and services, but in our discussion of these phenomena,[6] we are particularly interested in showing that something like externalities and economies of scale characterize redistribution and stabilization policies as well as the more familiar – at least to public finance economists – allocation policies, and hence use the words interactions and interdependencies instead of the more usual language of externalities and economies of scale to characterize these phenomena.

All the models analysed in this book are built on the idea that the amount of resources allocated to administration, co-ordination, mobility, and signalling varies as the structure of the public sector is varied. Because of the importance of this last concept in our work, we devote a large part of Chapter 3 to the formulation of a definition of the structure of the public sector and discuss how this structure can be represented by a scalar.

Having provided ourselves with a measure of the structure of the public sector, we formulate different models of how the constituent assembly – the body which we assume makes all the decisions about the structure of the public sector and to which we devote Chapter 6 – chooses a given structure. The models we examine fall in two broad classes. In one, the members of the constituent assembly are imagined to act in such a way as to minimize the amount of resources used up by citizens acting in their own interest, that is, seeking to improve their level of utility, and by governing politicians also seeking maximum utility. These models constitute Chapter 7.

In a second class of models, the members of the constituent assembly are assumed to be elected politicians and their advisers are assumed to be bureaucrats. The structure of the public sector which they choose is one which maximizes the utility of these two groups subject to a number of constraints which are defined and analysed in Chapter 8.

We can now indicate how our models of the structure of the public sector relate to those explanations of federalism which rest on the presence of linguistic, racial, religious, and / or other similar diversities. That relationship is easy to define. Diversities may, and often do, increase the costs of mobility, possibly that of signalling, and certainly that of co-ordination and administration activities. Diversities of that nature therefore imply that the organizational costs of two otherwise similar public sector structures will be different, being higher in the structure characterized by diversities.

4 OUTLINE

We have already indicated to the reader the general construction of our book. It may prove useful, however, to set out that outline in more detail.

Chapters 2 and 3 deal with definitions and assumptions. The first of the two presents a classification of the items – which we call functions or powers – which the constituent assembly assigns to each jurisdictional level and examines the interactions and interdependencies which characterize each one of them. Chapter 3 defines jurisdictions and jurisdictional levels, and then, as already indicated, provides a definition and a summary measure of the structure of the public sector. This chapter also introduces the constituent assembly, defines the institutional framework for the workings of our models, and sharpens the notion of organizational activities as it pertains to these models.

In Chapter 4, we provide a summary of the orthodox economic approach to federalism – we even extend it in some directions – and indicate why it is an unacceptable model of the assignment problem in federal states.

We then move on to Part Two, which begins with two chapters in which we introduce a number of hypotheses about the various actors in the public sector: citizens, politicians, and bureaucrats in alternative roles. Chapters 7 and 8 develop what we call least-cost and representative-government models of federalism. These two chapters contain in general terms our models of the assignment of functions to the various jurisdictional levels that constitute a federal state.

The discussion in Part Three is addressed to certain special topics. One of its main tasks is to show that the models of Part Two, which are formulated in general terms, apply to redistribution and stabilization as much as to allocation powers. As things now stand, it is customary to have an *ad hoc* model for redistribution, another one for stabilization, and a third more involved model, based on first principles, for the allocation functions.[7] Another purpose of Part Three, which gives rise to Chapter 12, is to present the view of intergovernmental grants which follows from the models of our book. At present, the theory of grants is based on a primitive view of governments and is independent of the model of the assignment of powers in federal states. It is largely an *ad hoc* theory. We hope to help remedy this state of affairs.

---

7 For a good illustration of this way of approaching the problem, see Wallace E. Oates, *Fiscal Federalism* (New York: Harcourt Brace Jovanovitch 1972).

2

Private activities, public policies, and jurisdictional functions

In this chapter, we examine some characteristics of the five classes of functions or powers that are assigned to the various jurisdictional levels that constitute the public sector of a given society. To be specific, in the next section we suggest a classification of functions and briefly illustrate the content of each class, then in Section 3 we focus on the geographical or spatial aspect of the functions and point to some essential features that are shared by all functions.

Before we introduce them, we should indicate that the definition of functions that we have adopted is fairly close to the everyday usage of that word. Indeed, we use it to refer to the power, responsibility, and authority that the government of a jurisdiction possesses to make decisions, to pursue policies, and to undertake activities in a particular area or in a specified domain once that power, responsibility, and authority has been assigned or given to a particular jurisdictional level (not to a jurisdiction *per se*, except in the case of the national jurisdiction when the jurisdictional level and the jurisdiction are co-terminous). The assignment of a function to a jurisdictional level is therefore a necessary condition for the governments of the jurisdictions at that level to have power to make decisions on the matters pertaining to that function.

We emphasize that *functions* must be distinguished from *policies*. Indeed, once a function has been assigned to a jurisdictional level, governments of jurisdictions at that level are free to make their own decisions about the quantity and character of their activities under that power, which includes, of course, the option of taking no action. This distinction between functions and policies will become more precise as we define and illustrate the various functions that are assigned in every public sector.

2 FIVE CLASSES OF FUNCTIONS

We must stress at the outset that the number of functions or domains of responsibility is large indeed. It is only because it is sometimes convenient and because it sometimes facilitates exposition that we group that large number into five classes or categories. When in the next chapter we introduce the notion of an assignment table – a simple device to describe and summarize the assignment of functions that exist at any point in time – we will use a complete, disaggregated list of all functions. Although, at other times, we will find it convenient to use the summary classification introduced in this chapter, we must always bear in mind that if we work with the summary classification it is easy to lose sight of the essential diversity of functions. To say that regulatory functions, for example, have been assigned to the national or to the provincial jurisdictional level would be misleading, unless it were meant that every conceivable regulatory power had been assigned to one or the other level.

We classify all functions under the following five headings: (a) regulatory functions, (b) supply functions, (c) revenue functions, (d) redistribution functions, and (e) stabilization functions. As anyone familiar with the economic literature knows, this is not a new system of classification and, though it may sometimes have been given a too exclusively economic content, it is quite a simple matter to broaden the interpretation to include all domains of power and authority, as we show below.

The regulatory functions pertain to such domains as abortion, censorship, currency, foreign trade, fisheries, immigration, transportation, weights and measures, etc. Regulatory functions encompass policies and decisions that assist, direct, guide, and govern the production, exchange, and distribution of goods in the private sector, as well as the administration of justice, civil rights, free speech, etc.

Decisions related to the kind of abortions that should be legalized, to the kind and extent of censorship, to whether a currency should be decimalized, and decisions about tariff rates, about the admission of potential immigrants, about the use of certain fishing gears, and about the adoption of the metric system are all *policies* that can be implemented if the *power* or responsibility has been conferred on a government by the assignment of the particular regulatory function.

Functions are also assigned which empower public expenditures on certain goods and services. These we call supply functions. They include expenditures on the armed forces, on lighthouses, education, public schools, hospitals, and street cleaning – to name but a few. Supply and regulatory functions are sometimes treated together under the heading of allocation functions.[1] There is no harm in

---

1 See, for example, Wallace E. Oates, *Fiscal Federalism* (New York: Harcourt Brace Jovanovitch 1972).

doing this and we would certainly have adopted this latter nomenclature if we had not observed that the assignment of regulatory functions is often forgotten when they are lumped in with supply.

The third type of functions – the revenue functions – is the power to command not only the collection of monetary revenues or taxes, but the direct levy of goods and services. One can classify taxes according to their base: it is possible, for example, to distinguish between taxes on profits, on personal incomes, on payrolls, on sales, on property, on inheritances, and on other bases. If one operates with this distinction, then the right to use the income base is a function, while what we call policy concerns the details of rate, exemption, time of payment, enforcement, and so forth.

The revenue functions also include the power or right to impose fines, to draft individuals for the armed forces, or to fight forest fires, or for some other special purpose task forces. It also includes the right of expropriation, forcing private owners of property to sell. In these special cases, the 'revenue' that accrues to the state is the net value of the goods, services, or assets 'commandeered.'

The discussion of the preceeding paragraph illustrates how difficult it sometimes is to distinguish between certain powers, especially when it is desired to sort them in broad classes. If, for example, a government has the power to require the use of seat-belts in cars, or to require the use of minimum size lots for residential construction, we can say that it has the power to regulate, but we could also say that it has the power to force the expenditure of money by private citizens, and hence that it possesses certain revenue functions. There is no way of preventing these difficulties from arising; one must simply be aware of them, and seek to avoid the pitfalls to which they give rise.

Finally, in addition to the power to collect taxes and to 'commandeer' goods and services, the revenue functions include the power to impose fees and user charges, as well as the power to sell bonds and to borrow generally.

The fourth class of functions, redistribution, is less easy than the first three to define. The term has a number of meanings. In one sense it refers to an intention to change the distribution of income or wealth among a group of persons, or in favour of a group of recipients. In another, it refers to the power to use a specific instrument of redistribution.

The first meaning can be illustrated either by the choice of rates of tax on persons with high incomes, or by the exemption from tax of a good used by persons with low incomes. Such policies, which are simply modifications of policies carried out under supply or revenue powers, are different from policies carried out under explicitly redistributive functions, such as (*a*) the making of formula-type payments like old-age support, unemployment insurance, and family allowances; (*b*) discretionary or discriminating payments such as public assistance and welfare; and (c) services in kind like health and medical services, manpower and educational services, free public housing subsidies, and disaster relief. It can be seen, however, that these functions merge into the first three classifications, becoming difficult to distinguish from them and from (d) the making of grants to poor communities and (e) the replacement of a proportional by a progressive income tax.

The position taken in this study is that, in general, redistributive powers can be distinguished from the supply and regulatory functions by the intent rather than by the method or instrument used in policy decisions. Our treatment in a later chapter, Chapter 10, is based on this distinction. However, we shall base most of our discussion on the simplifying assumption that redistribution is carried out by the use of specific redistributive instruments.[2] As a consequence, old age pensions, free hospitalization, and 'welfare' are functions to be assigned.

The fifth and final class of functions is concerned with the stabilization of macro-aggregate dimensions of the economy. As with distribution, these functions are better identified by the intention than by the power to use a specialized set of stabilization instruments. The stabilization functions would then relate to the power to engage in certain actions with the intention of stabilizing any number of aggregate magnitudes, such as the level of output, the level of employment, the level of prices, etc. as well as the rate of change in these aggregate magnitudes. Though stabilization functions are defined by intent with respect to macro-dimensions, the instruments used by governments are certainly not restricted to any textbook list of macro-economic policy instruments; some micro-economic instruments can also be employed. We discuss this subject in Chapter 11.

In the remainder of this section, we seek to demonstrate that all activities and policies, whether they pertain to the regulatory, supply, revenue, redistribution, or to the stabilization functions display a common property of interaction or interdependence which we label spill-overs and externalities for certain activities, empathy for others, and leakages for still others. Below, we shall examine the features of the interactions that characterize each class of functions.

Our reason for discussing these externalities and other similar phenomena in a book which proposes a theory of the structure of the public sector based on 'or-

---

2 An alternative position is that redistribution is the aim of a 'branch' or 'budget' of the government. This branch may be envisaged as reviewing all supply, regulatory, and revenue decisions, and remedying their distributive results. We feel that this assumption is not only artificial but misleading in that it implies the conclusion that every government at each jurisdictional level (national, provincial, local, etc.) must have its own redistributive branch. This seems to avoid the assignment problem. Furthermore, it is a mystery to us that Musgrave and others that follow him in this approach could also have insisted that redistribution be assigned only to the central government.

ganizational' activities rather than on spill-overs is that the two are related. Indeed, in our approach spill-overs are one of the principal influences that give rise to 'organizational' activities. The reader who doubts this need only recall that 'organizational' activities include co-ordination between governments and co-ordination is necessary to mitigate, or compensate, for the effects of externalities.

Regulatory and supply functions
The interactions that are specific to supply and regulatory functions are the spillovers, externalities, degree of publicness of public goods, and congestion associated with these phenomena which one encounters in the literature of public finance and welfare economics. It is not necessary therefore to devote much space to them because their main properties are well known to the reader.

To be brief, assume that the benefits (positive or negative) from a public policy or from the actions of a private citizen, firm, or government are not fully appropriated by the individual, firm, or government providing the policy or engaging in the action, but spill over to other individuals, firms, or governments. Imagine further that the flow of spill-overs can be represented by a curve in Cartesian space, where one dimension of that space (the horizontal one) is the number of people, somehow arrayed[3], and the other is the amount or value (in money or in utility) of the spill-over.[4] Such span curves can be positively or negatively sloped, monotone or not, and therefore include the familiar case of rectangular distributions. The horizontal length of these curves tells us how many people are affected by a given spill-over – we call this the span of a policy or of an activity – while the height of the curves portray the value or amount of the spill-over, of that span.

Everything we have said above about the spillovers of regulatory and supply activities applies also to the interactions from economies of scale. Indeed, as is well known, there is nothing in principle that distinguishes these from externalities or public goods.

Revenue functions
The nature of the interdependence in the case of the revenue functions depends on the shifting and incidence of taxes. Consequently, the span of a tax or the extent of its interaction will depend on whether it is levied on an origin or destination principle, on the extent to which remissions are allowed, and particularly on the geographical mobility of goods and services and of factors of production. In

---

3 The array will vary with the phenomena studied and is therefore largely an empirical question.
4 See Figure 4.1 in Chapter 4 for such a diagram.

other words, the configuration of the interaction will be determined by the forces that are analysed in the theories of tax incidence, border taxes (tariffs), and border tax adjustment.[5]

As with regulatory and supply functions, the incidence of a tax need not give rise to a span curve that is monotone, so that scallops and wiggles of various size and magnitude can be expected. It is not possible, however, to deny that the spatial impact of taxes is a subject about which even less is known than about tax incidence generally.

Redistribution functions[6]
To the extent that a redistributional policy takes the form of supplying a public good that will be enjoyed mostly by the poor, or to the extent that such a policy consists in adjusting taxes whose incidence is borne either by the rich or by the poor, the analysis conducted above applies without change. In other words, whether the motivation for providing a public good or for adjusting taxes is allocational or redistributive has no effect on the span of policies and consequently leaves the extent of interaction unchanged.

When redistribution is motivated by utility interdependence or 'empathy' for particular persons, new forms of interaction have to be considered. Vickrey and Boulding have described how philanthropic feelings may be viewed as forms of economic interdependence, and these views have been used and applied to certain contexts by writers on Pareto-optimal redistribution.[7] While these authors have pictured redistribution as government-organized transfers from individual donors to other individuals, they have paid little attention to the empathy span underlying this process.[8]

We may borrow Vickrey's word 'empathy' to describe a surface defined over individuals' incomes, declining with 'distance' from a particular citizen or from his government. It is easiest to think of 'distance' in geographical terms, the as-

5 On the distinction between the last two, see H.G. Johnson and M. Krauss, 'Border Taxes, Border Tax Adjustments, Comparative Advantage, and the Balance of Payments,' *Canadian Journal of Economics* III 4 (November 1970).

6 Some of the special problems that arise in assigning the redistribution functions to jurisdictional levels are discussed at greater length in Chapter 10.

7 See William S. Vickrey, 'One Economist's View of Philanthropy,' and Kenneth E. Boulding, 'Notes on a Theory of Philanthropy,' in Frank G. Dickinson, ed., *Philanthropy and Public Policy* (New York: National Bureau of Economic Research 1962), and H.M. Hochman and J.D. Rodgers, 'Pareto Optimal Redistribution,' *American Economic Review* (September 1969).

8 In M.V. Pauly, 'Income Redistribution as a Local Public Good,' *Journal of Public Economics* II, 1 (February 1973) 43ff, 'concern' for the poor does taper off in discontinuous steps, jurisdiction by jurisdiction.

sumption being that citizens' awareness of gaps between their incomes and those of other persons tends to diminish spatially. But in a more detailed treatment, 'distance' would be rendered as a complex measure that takes into account age, race, culture, family, cultural, and religious connections, the citizen's recent travels, and other sources of information about the interest in persons in remote areas.[9] In this case the degree of empathy defines the span of the good called redistribution.

Stabilization functions[10]

If stabilization of the macro-aggregates of an economy is attempted by the implementation of such policies as the control or regulation of prices, wages, and interest rates or by redistributing income, the nature of the extent of interaction will be as described in the earlier sub-sections of this chapter. Nothing more need be added, since in these cases one wants to focus on the incidence of these regulatory mechanisms.

If, however, stabilization is attempted through the operation of monetary and fiscal policy, interdependence must be defined with the help of spatial multipliers such as those defined in international balance of payments theory. To put it in its simplest form, assume a situation of equilibrium, that is a situation in which the balance of payments of every area or jurisdiction is in equilibrium. If the government of one jurisdiction increases its expenditures by $1.00, that will generate an increase in imports from some of the other jurisdictions. This, in turn, will increase the first jurisdiction's exports and hence its income.

In this case, the vertical axis in the space used to portray the extent of interaction measures the size of the leakages resulting from the unit increase in expenditures, and the span, measured horizontally, indicates the number of persons affected by that increase.

4 CONCLUSION

We have argued in the last section that every class of functions is associated with a particular kind of interaction linking citizens, firms, and / or governments. We have further argued that for every class of functions the span and the intensity of these interactions can be depicted by a curve relating the amount or value of spill-

9 'Distance' may not be independent of jurisdictional boundary lines. Persons may have a greater concern for the incomes of their fellow citizens in their own jurisdiction than for the income of 'foreigners,' even if the latter live closer to them. This could justify Pauly's measure of distance in terms of jurisdictions.

10 The reader is referred to Chapter 11 for an extended discussion of the assignment of the stabilization functions.

overs, etc., to the number of citizens affected. Since the array of citizens on the horizontal axis is essentially empirical, so is the definition of spans. However, the fact that the notions of span and interaction can be applied to all classes of powers indicates that the theory developed in this book applies to all functions.

In addition, this common feature of functions makes it possible for us to treat the various organizational activities of citizens and governments – signalling, mobility, administration, and co-ordination – in general terms, that is, without asking whether the co-ordination activities of governments, for example, apply only to the allocation functions and not to the other functions. To put it differently, the fact that all classes of functions display interactions of one kind or another means that we do not need one model for the assignment of regulatory and supply functions, another model for the assignment of redistribution functions, and a third for the assignment of stabilization functions, as is usual in the literature. As should become evident to the reader, one theory will do for all of these – and also for the revenue functions, which usually are not even mentioned!

3

Structural dimensions of the public sector

1 INTRODUCTION

Now that we have stated what we mean by functions and policies, we will, after defining jurisdictions and jurisdictional levels, develop a concept that will play a central role in our theory of the structure of the public sector because it will be our representation or measure of that structure: the assignment table. We will then suggest an index or summary measure, albeit an imperfect one, of that table, which we will call the degree of centralization; we will present, as illustrations, some tentative numbers on the behaviour of that co-efficient for Canada, Switzerland, and the United States.

As will become clear later on, we will assume throughout that decisions about the structure of the public sector are taken by a body that we call the constituent assembly, and which we introduce in Section 5. In Section 6, we list the assumptions that we make about the institutional framework in which decisions are made and finally, in Section 7, we define the organizational activities that characterize the behaviour of citizens and governments operating in the public sector.

2 JURISDICTIONS AND JURISDICTIONAL LEVELS

While our use of the words functions and policies accords well with what is familiar, this is not quite the case with our definition of jurisdictions. In common parlance, these are often used as synonyms for governments. Our terminology may cover that usage, but we will at once extend the meaning of the word to refer to potential public bodies, and restrict it to include only those bodies that have to account directly or indirectly for at least some of their decisions through mechanisms such as elections.

For example, the provinces of New Brunswick, Nova Scotia, and Prince Edward Island are each jurisdictions in the commonly accepted sense of the word, but the Maritime Provinces as a whole is also a jurisdiction in our sense, since one or more functions could potentially be assigned to a body or institution with responsibility to the population of the area now encompassed by the three provinces. Such bodies are often called 'special purpose' authorities or governments in the institutional and legal literature on the subject. Actual school boards and potential consolidated or fragmented school boards that serve populations of areas that are not necessarily co-terminous with any other jurisdiction provide another example.

It must be stressed that to be classifiable as a jurisdiction in our sense a body cannot be a simple administrative or bureaucratic entity, neither can it be a special co-ordinating device between governments; it must be responsible to an electorate of citizens which has the ultimate power of denying re-election or of re-electing the members of that body. The United Nations, made up of delegates of member countries, is not a jurisdiction in our sense of the word. *A fortiori*, co-ordinating and administrative agencies such as the International Joint Commission, the Tennessee Valley Authority, or the National Harbours Board are not jurisdictions for the purpose of the following analysis.

We define levels of jurisdictions in terms of population or territory as an aggregation of jurisdictions. As is implied by the words, the idea of jurisdictional level is intimately related to that of position or height by exclusive reference to the population or territory of other levels. Therefore a jurisdictional level is higher than another when it includes more than one jurisdiction of the other level. For example, a national level is higher than a provincial one because it includes more than one provincial jurisdiction. However, a municipal level may or may not be higher than a school district; it will depend on whether the municipality encompasses several school districts or *vice versa*.

The reader should note that this definition does not require that higher-level jurisdictions be assigned more functions, or be in any other way more important than lower-level jurisdictions, except in terms of territory and population. Nor does it imply that lower level jurisdictions be tributaries to, or creatures of, a higher-level jurisdiction.

3 THE ASSIGNMENT TABLE

Using the complete list of functions – not the summary five-way classification – and that of jurisdictional levels, we draw up a list of all functions and a list of all actual *and* potential jurisdictional levels and bring these together in the form of a table such as that displayed in Figure 3.1.

	f_1	f_2					f_β				f_r
J_1	0	0	1	0	0	0	0	1	1	0	0
J_2			1				0				0
•	1	0	0	0	0	0	0	0	0	0	0
•							1				0
•	0	0	0	0	0	0	0	0	0	0	0
J_δ							1				0
•							1				0
•							1				0
•							1				0
J_q							1				0

Figure 3.1

The rows on the table refer to the various jurisdictional levels J_δ ($\delta = 1, \ldots q$), while the columns depict the functions (including, of course, the revenue functions) $f_\beta (\delta = 1, \ldots r)$. To illustrate, J_1 could be the whole of Canada; J_2 could be the provincial level made up of one set of combinations of the present ten provinces, such as the five-regional set now often used in presenting Canadian statistical data; J_3 to J_8 could be other sets of provincial combinations; J_9 could be the present ten provinces; J_{10} to J_{50} could be various potential divisions of the present ten provinces to constitute an intermediate level or levels below the present provincial level; J_{51} to J_{101} could be various combinations of the units at the municipal level in each of the provinces today, while J_{102} to some higher number could be counties, school districts, etc.

To obtain an assignment table, we simply need two symbols to indicate whether a function has or has not been assigned to a jurisdictional level. We use 0 to indicate that a function has not been placed under the responsibility of a given jurisdictional level – and consequently assigned to the jurisdictions that constitute that level – and 1 to signify that it has.

The reader should note that in any one column there can be more than one 1, since the same function can be assigned to more than one jurisdictional level; this joint occupation of a field has sometimes been given the name of 'concurrent authority.' In addition, one expects that a number of rows in a given table will contain only zeros, since, in general, there will be potential jurisdictional levels which are not active. Similarly, a column could be made up exclusively of zeros if a function had not been assigned to any jurisdictional level.[1] All these possibil-

1 Because of the existence of general and residual clauses like responsibility for 'peace, order, and good government' to be found embedded in most constitutions, there is a

ities are illustrated in Figure 3.1. It need hardly be stressed that, as defined, a particular table does not represent an assignment that is either an equilibrium or an optimal one. A table is simply a way of describing one structure of the public sector.

4 THE DEGREE OF CENTRALIZATION

To simplify our task in the chapters ahead we have devised an index of the degree of centralization, which we use as a summary of the particular assignment table that is observable in each period. Our aim was to provide a measure that has a higher value if the structure of the public sector corresponds to an intuitive notion of 'centralization' and a low value if that structure is decentralized. We believe that for expository purposes such an index is a convenience. However, we believe that in any practical inquiry in the structure of a public sector, especially when concerned with non-supply functions, a full assignment table will often be used. An index merely simplifies our task in the next few chapters, and what follows, with all its defects, is presented exclusively for that purpose.

We proceed as follows. First, we assume that the boundaries of lower-level jurisdictions never cross the boundaries of higher-level jurisdictions, so that it is always possible to say that the former are entirely enclosed within the latter. Second, because our index of the degree of centralization (γ) applies only to observable assignment tables, we construct an index that is a weighted average of all the jurisdictional levels to which functions are actually assigned. The weights chosen are total expenditures at each level, regardless of the functions on which money is spent. Jurisdictional levels are defined in terms of the population (or territory) of a typical jurisdiction at that level. Hence variation in the value of the index is due to variation in the size of the jurisdictions to which functions have been assigned.[2]

To be more specific, assume that in Figure 3.1, we enter, instead of the 1's, the exact amount of money spent on the assigned functions in a period that we use as a base.[3] Then we add the expenditures horizontally for each row and in this way collapse the entire table to a single column. Each row total is then mul-

sense in which all conceivable functions are always assigned. A column of zeros therefore merely indicates that some function in a concrete and well-described version has not been explicitly assigned.

2 The index might also be adapted to give weight to the amount of private expenditure *regulated* at each level of jurisdiction. That is not attempted here.

3 The existence of concurrent authority and of conditional grants between levels poses a difficulty for the practical application of the index. The user must decide how much of a total expenditure under a particular function is to be imputed to each level. In principle, each level's weight should reflect its fraction of the power to alter total expenditure under that function.

tiplied by the population of that row, ie, of the typical jurisdictional unit at that level, and then divided by the total expenditures of the public sector of that society times its total population.

If we let E stand for expenditures, P_δ for the population of a typical unit at jurisdictional level δ, and P for total population, then our index of centralization is:

$$\gamma^1 = \left[\sum_{\beta=1}^{r} \sum_{\delta=1}^{q} (E^1_{\beta\delta} P^1_\delta) \right] \Big/ \left[P^0 \sum_{\beta=1}^{r} \sum_{\delta=1}^{q} E^0_{\beta\delta} \right]$$

where the superscripts denote time periods or different societies depending on what it is that one wishes to compare.

The index is designed to summarize the structure of a public sector in one period relative to another, so that comparisons of γ's for two or more assignment tables will indicate the direction of change of the weighted average of the levels at which activity is carried out. This is illustrated in columns 1 to 4 of Table 3.1. The entries show the distribution of $400 (million) of expenditure between four jurisdictional levels numbered 1 to 4. Calculated values of γ for each of the four cases are shown in the bottom row of the table. For the population sizes and expenditure numbers used, an equal distribution of expenditures across the four jurisdictional levels produces a γ of 0.273. If all expenditure is done at the national level, $\gamma = 1.000$, and if all is at the parish level, $\gamma = .0001$.

The first four cases therefore show how changing the expenditure weights (which we may assume represents changing the assignment of functions) alters the value of γ in a way that accords with ordinary usage.

The next two cases (columns 5 and 6) show how γ changes when the weight structure *within* each of the four jurisdictional levels changes, the total expenditure weight for each level remaining the same as in Case 1. It will be seen that simply dividing each of the twelve provinces (in Case 1) into four states, giving us a total of 48 states, leads to a *fall* in γ, even if all activity at the second level is unchanged. In Column 6, only half of Case 1's twelve provinces are subdivided into four states; the decline in γ is smaller than in Case 5.

Cases 7 to 11 show that γ does respond to minor redistributions of expenditure among intermediate-level jurisdictions. Case 10 shows that a large percentage increase (from Case 6) in spending at the parish level at the expense of the provincial level reduces the index only slightly; this may be compared with Case 11 where it is seen that a similar percentage decrease in expenditure at the national level leads to a more pronounced fall in γ. These illustrations suggest that γ varies in ways that accord with an everyday notion of centralization.[4] The *magnitudes*

4 See R.A. Musgrave and P.B. Musgrave, *Public Finance in Theory and Practice* (New

Table 3.1
Values of $\Sigma_\beta \Sigma_\delta E_{\beta\delta}$ for alternative assignment tables

Jurisdictional level	Number of jurisdictions	Size of P_δ	1	2	3	4	5	6	7	8	9	10	11
1	1 national	240	100	400	200	0	100	100	100	100	100	100	50
2	12 provinces	20	100	0	150	0							
	48 states	5					100						
	6 provinces	20						50	70	30	50	50	50
	24 states	5						50	30	70	10	10	60
3	120 cities	2	100	0	25	0	100	100	100	100		100	150
	60 cities	2									50		
	60 cities	2									90		
4	960 parishes	25	100	0	25	400	100	100	100	100	100	140	90
	γ		0.273	1.000	0.529	0.001	0.257	0.265	0.268	0.262	0.264	0.263	0.139

of the changes have less significance, depending as they do on the numbers we have chosen for the illustrations.

Another way to understand our index of centralization is to apply it to the phenomenon of shifting population (or public output) between two adjoining jurisdictions. Some recent work[5] has been concerned with the optimal distribution of goods or people between two sides of a boundary. In that literature, there is no question of assigning functions to higher or lower levels, or even of subdividing a level. In effect, the search is for the optimal location of the boundary. We may ask when such a shift in the boundary (or of people and public output) should be called centralizing, and how it would be described by our index.

Again, intuition suggests that, if a change in boundary concentrates more people or more activity into a jurisdiction that is already large, it would be termed centralizing. If, on the contrary, it transfers people or activity towards a smaller jurisdiction, it would be decentralizing. Somewhat the same result is obtained by our index. Assume that the effect of a boundary shift is to move a certain number of people out of j_2 into j_1. Then, using base period weights, γ increases or decreases according as $\Sigma_\delta E_{\delta j_1} \gtrless \Sigma_\delta E_{\delta j_2}$ and as $P_1 \gtrless P_2$.

York: McGraw-Hill 1973) 622-8, for one way of indexing the extent of decentralization. For another, see A. Maass, ed., *Area and Power: A Theory of Local Government* (Glencoe: Free Press 1959) 10. A third way would involve an adaptation of the Herfindahl index.

5 J.M. Buchanan and R. Wagner, 'An Efficiency Basis for Federal Fiscal Equalization,' in National Bureau of Economic Research, J. Margolis, ed., *The Analysis of Public Output* (New York: Columbia University Press 1970) 139-58; F. Flatters, V. Henderson, and P. Mieszkowski, 'Public Goods, Efficiency, and Regional Fiscal Equalization,' *Journal of Public Economics* III 2 (May 1974) 99-112

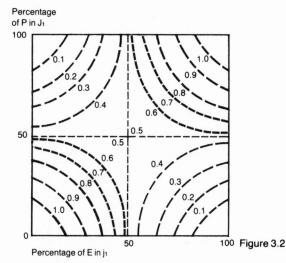

Percentage
of P in j_1

Percentage of E in j_1

Figure 3.2

The pattern of dependence is sketched in Figure 3.2. It is assumed that there are only two jurisdictions, and that the expenditures used to weight γ are those of the base period. The vertical axis represents the percentage of total population, P, in the society who reside in j_1 (the distance to 100 must then represent those residing in j_2). The horizontal axis represents the percentage of the total expenditure of the two jurisdictions that is undertaken by j_1. The broken line contours (including the central straight lines) are values of γ.

To illustrate, choose an initial point anywhere in the figure. A transfer of population to j_1 means that from the initial point, one moves upwards. Then if the initial position was to the left of the 50 per cent expenditure line, that upward move lowers γ; if it was to the right, the move raises it.

It is also possible to examine the effect on γ of a change in both population and expenditure. If the result of mobility is that j_1 gains in its percentages of both total population and expenditure, we move diagonally upward through the figure. The effect on γ as always will depend on the initial position. In general, if j_1 is small in both dimensions, any small gain of population and expenditure reduces γ, while if it is large in both dimensions, small gains increase γ.

Note that here we use γ differently than we did in Cases 1 to 4 of Table 3.1. There we kept the expenditure weights at each of the four jurisdictional levels constant. Here, examining a change within the structure of one level, we allow both P_δ and E_δ to change. Both uses of the measure are legitimate.

We have shown that given any assignment table, it is possible, by using base period weights, to devise a scalar measure of the table which behaves much as our intuition tells us it should behave. One problem with which we have not dealt is that even if a unique value of γ can be attached to any assignment table, the reverse is not true: for any γ, there exist many assignment tables. This means that beginning with some initial assignment table for which we calculate a value of γ, a reassignment which produces a specific change in γ will not be associated with a unique assignment table.

That is a serious theoretical problem for which we have no solution.[6] In practice, the problem may not be as serious as implied. There is first the fact that as a rule γ is not likely to change substantially in any period, so that it may be quite easy, given the initial assignment table and corresponding γ, to find the value of the new table associated with the altered γ. Second, one observes that functions are often reassigned without changing the boundaries of jurisdictions or alternatively that changes in boundaries occur without any corresponding changes in the assignment of functions. When the assignment table changes in this way – that is, when only one dimension at a time changes – and when base period weights are held constant, a γ will usually be associated with a unique assignment table. In any case, as we already pointed out, a summary measure of assignment tables is primarily an expository device; in applied work, the assignment itself would often be used. Nevertheless, we thought the reader could be interested in the actual behaviour of the centralization co-efficient for particular countries. Consequently we have done some simple calculations for Canada, the United States, and more limited ones for Switzerland. Data for three levels – federal, state, and municipal – exist also for Germany and Australia, but we have not done any calculations for them.

We have confined ourselves to the twentieth century, as earlier data are not uniform. The use of national accounts definitions for such concepts as expenditures on goods and services and transfer payments has helped to insure intertemporal and international consistency, though we are well aware of the problems involved in such comparisons.[7]

The form given to the co-efficient allows us to make two types of comparison: one in which base-year expenditures are used as fixed weights and the structures of populations as the indicators; and a second type in which the base-year structures of populations are used as weights and changing expenditures at each level as indicators. Because the relative population structure (number of levels and number of jurisdictions at each level) changes very gradually over time, the first type of index has been very nearly constant over time since the early part of the century. Thus the chief value of this type is for making international comparisons, some of which are shown in Table 3.2.

6 The problem is a pervasive one. For example, though each Lorenz curve is associated with one Gini co-efficient, each co-efficient is associated with a family of Lorenz curves.

7 For each country, we calculated the populations of states, provinces, and municipalities

Table 3.2
Values of γ for Canada, US, and Switzerland, for various years, using fixed expenditure weights

	Expenditures on goods and services		Transfers (including debt services)		Total expenditures	
	1927	1972	1927	1972	1927	1972
United States						
1900	.264	.433	.570	.805	.299	.522
1926	.263	.433	.510	.805	.299	.522
1972	.263	.432	.510	.805	.299	.522
Canada						
1926	.273	.322	.573	.676	.384	.432
1972	.271	.318	.570	.673	.381	.429
Switzerland	(1952)		(1952)		(1952)	
1952	.434	.359	.397	.119	.430	.328
1972	.434	.359	.597	.119	.430	.328

In this table the columns show the source of the weights, the year chosen for the base, and the kind of government expenditure. The rows show the years (and country) for which the structure of jurisdictions are being indexed. Thus the first value in the table for both Canada and the United States shows the co-efficient based on the population structure of jurisdictions in the earliest year available, using their structure of expenditures in 1927 as the weights. Using these early weights, the degree of centralization of Canada is shown always to have been very slightly greater than in the United States, a situation which still prevailed in 1972. The same relationship is seen to emerge from calculations in which transfer payments (including interest on the public debt) and total government expenditures are used as weights.

However, when weights are derived from the structure of expenditures in 1972,

by dividing the national population by the number of jurisdictions at each level. For example, in 1950, the 'urban' population figure was about 75,000 in Canada and 100,000 in the US. Detailed sources on populations and outlays were as follows:
United States: *Historical Statistics of the U.S.; Statistical Abstract of the United States* (various years); Bureau of Census: *1972 Census of Governments Vol. 6, No. 4* and *Government Finances* (various years); *Economic Report of the President*, 1974.
Canada: Statistics Canada, *National Accounts, Income and Expenditures*, Numbers 13-502 and 13-533; *Canadian Statistical Review*, 11-505; and *Canada Year Book* (various years)
Switzerland: *Statistisches Jahrbüch der Schweiz* (various years). Note: the Swiss data do not accord with national accounts definitions.

the two countries' indexes of centralization reverse their order and pull well apart, especially for transfer-payment weights; the value for Canada is about 0.67, and that for the US is about 0.80. Both countries tend to centralize interest payments and welfare transfers more than they do goods and services (and much more than Switzerland does), but the US's recent tendency in this direction is especially significant.

The extent of a tendency towards centralization can best be detected by using the second type of comparison, in which the population structure of a given year is used to weight the changing expenditures at each level. For the three countries, the weights are the jurisdictional populations of the latest year, 1972. (The use of 1952 or 1927 population weights does change the absolute levels of the index, but not their pattern, nor their inter-country ranking.)

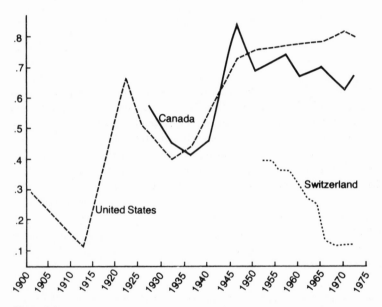

Figure 3.3

Figures 3.3 and 3.4 present the most interesting comparisons, suggesting the general similarity of the three federations' centralization of expenditures, and the great differences in their centralization of transfer payments. Values of γ for transfers only (including interest on the public debt) are shown in Figure 3.3. It can be seen (a) that since World War II both Canada and the United States have had highly centralized transfer systems, but that their degrees of centralization

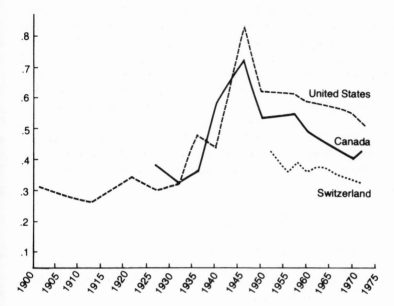

Figure 3.4

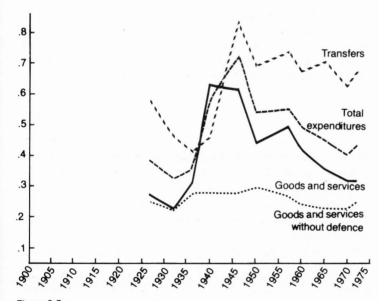

Figure 3.5

are now slowly diverging, presumably in response to Canada's tendency to assign welfare and other systems to the provinces; and (*b*) that the Swiss transfer system is, in comparison, highly decentralized.

Figure 3.4 shows total government expenditures (including transfers and all defence expenditures). Among the interesting details are the New Deal (central) expenditure hump in the US; not quite matched in Canada, and the recent decline in over-all centralization (even with the US's Vietnam spending) in all three countries.

Figure 3.5 shows four curves for Canada only. It is interesting that the lowest curve, for all non-defence goods and services (ie, excluding both transfers and military expenditures), has kept a nearly constant low level of centralization since 1926.[8]

5 CONSTITUENT ASSEMBLIES

Constituent assemblies are bodies made up of individuals whose tasks as members of these assemblies we restrict to designing the boundaries of jurisdictions and to assigning the functions or powers to jurisdictional levels. In doing so, assemblies *ipso facto* determine what the assignment table will be.

Constituent assemblies come in many forms and varieties and the rules which govern their conduct are also numerous and changing. To get specific results about a particular assignment problem, it will consequently be necessary to be specific about the kind of constituent assembly which is presumed to exist and about the rules of behaviour which govern the members of that particular assembly. We devote a full chapter – Chapter 6 – to a discussion of these problems. The definition given above will be sufficient for the intervening discussion.

6 THE INSTITUTIONAL FRAMEWORK

Like all economic theories, the one developed in this book depends on some assumption or other concerning the institutional framework within which behaviour takes place. While recognizing that this framework may itself be an endogenous component of a wider and more ambitious theory, it is imperative to set limits even if these are somewhat arbitrary. The usefulness of our model depends on the invariance of our assumed institutional framework relative to the variability of the endogenous elements.

There are three characteristics of the institutional framework which we take

8 These calculations have been augmented by others in which we have exchanged US and Canadian weights and have examined the US pattern without defence. (The latter curve is not like the Canadian non-defence index in Figure 3.5, but rises parallel below the US total curve.)

as given, not in the sense that they will remain invariant for the whole of the analysis, but in the sense that changes in them will be exogenous to the model presented here. These characteristics pertain (*a*) to the franchise, (*b*) to the decision rules for electing governments, and (*c*) to the nature of governing institutions.

We present no theory of the extent to which a population is enfranchised. We simply take the extent of the franchise as given. The proportion of the population that is enfranchised as well as the rules of enfranchisement can vary from one jurisdictional level to another; we do not assume that they are laid down by our constituent assembly. For example, one jurisdictional level may give automatic franchise to everyone who is 18 years of age and over, while another level restricts the franchise to an older group of individuals who in addition satisfy a longer residence requirement, while another jurisdiction levies a poll tax or restricts the franchise to property owners, or to those who do not fail a literacy test, etc.

We assume also that the decision rules for choosing governments are exogenous. These rules specify whether decisions are to be made when a simple majority or a plurality or some proportion of the enfranchised population or of the voting population favours an outcome. Again, simple majority rules may obtain in one jurisdictional level, while proportionality of one kind or another or plurality obtains in another.

Lastly, we assume that in every jurisdiction the existing political institutions are those of representative democracy. This last concept is not an easy one to define, but for our purposes it will be assumed to exist when voters vote to choose representatives and do not vote directly on issues or on the amount of public goods to supply, when voters elect representatives to pre-stated institutions, when decisions on issues are made by the elected representatives or by individuals that are accountable to them, and finally when elections to decide whether an incumbent representative should be re-elected or replaced and whether an incumbent party or executive should remain in office take place at intervals set according to some rule. The theory of the structure of the public sector developed in this book does not therefore apply to all existing public structures – only to those that are democratic.

7 'ORGANIZATIONAL' ACTIVITIES OF CITIZENS AND GOVERNMENTS

To simplify the construction of a theory of the public sector, we have grouped into four general classes the 'organizational' activities in which citizens and governments engage. The activities that are particular to citizens we call *signalling* and *mobility*, and those particular to governments we label *administration* and *co-ordination*. It must be stressed that these four components of organizational activities are defined in such a way as to include all the organizational activities of the public sector. There are no others, and therefore any 'new' one must be classified under one or the other of the above headings.

Since one of us has already described activities in which citizens engage when they participate in the political process,[9] we restrict ourselves here to a listing of the various activities. In Chapter 5, we shall provide the motivation that induces citizens to engage in these activities.

Included in the activities that we call signalling are: '(1) participating in efforts to influence the actions of lobbies and large pressure groups; (2) engaging in actions to influence politicians directly; (3) joining social movements; (4) regulating one's own private economic behaviour; (5) organizing the private provision of public and non-private goods ... and (7) voting or the act of giving one's support to or withholding it from a candidate of a political party or, in very special cases, a policy.'[10] Under the heading of mobility, we list only, of course, the act of moving from one jurisdiction to another.

Governments, as we indicated above, also engage in two kinds of organizational activities: administration and co-ordination, or, if the reader prefers, internal and external (ie, interjurisdictional) co-ordination.

We use the term administration to cover a large number of activities. Under it we include setting up new legislatures and constructing new government buildings for new jurisdictions. We also include activities necessary for governments to select, implement, and oversee its policies; but we exclude the use of resources which constitute the policy output itself.

The one important aspect of administration activities is search, particularly (a) search for the preferences of citizens and (b) search for a method or a procedure – what can be called a technology – related to the formulation and implementation of policies.

Political parties may acquire information about preferences not only by means of discussion in legislatures and in caucuses and by holding elections, but also through the use of surveys, polls, delegations, and correspondence. If tastes were similar, search activity might be modest. However, if jurisdictions are set up in such a way as to encompass many voters whose preferences cannot easily be ascertained, political parties will be forced into extensive search activity. An increase in the number of functions assigned to a jurisdiction need not increase search activity proportionately, as information-gathering devices may have the capacity to ascertain preferences on many issues at once. Furthermore, if it is known that policies are highly complementary, the amount of search required to ascertain demand for them will be less than the amount that would be needed if they were independent.

9 A. Breton, *The Economic Theory of Representative Government* (Chicago: Aldine 1974) Chapter 5
10 Breton, *Economic Theory of Representative Government* 75. Activity (6) is mobility, which is dealt with separately.

Very closely related to the search for preferences and to be included with administrative activities are the actions of governments aimed at altering the preferences of citizens through political advertising. To the extent that such advertising is successful it makes search less costly.

Governments also engage in search aimed at learning about the technology of producing policies. By way of illustration, we can point to the periodic reviews of alternative defence technologies, ranging from the choice of weapons and size of the armed forces to the advisability of alliances and treaties. Less spectacular examples are the search for preferred or less expensive ways of delivering justice, medical care, literacy, highway safety, freedom from smog, and of collecting tax revenues. Governments also from time to time obtain information about the distribution of income (or the extent of poverty) and about alternative instruments of redistribution; about unemployment and inflation and the relation of unemployment insurance, private job search, and other stabilization instruments.

Search for preferences and for technology need not be confined to one jurisdiction. Governments will wish to know about tastes and technologies in adjoining jurisdictions, not only with an eye to bargaining on supply and regulation, but also to increase the effectiveness of their own policies about redistribution, taxation, and stabilization, especially if spatial spill-overs that transcend jurisdictional boundaries exist.

The second organizational activity of governments is (external) co-ordination. Co-ordination is necessary because of the spill-overs originating with private activities and government policies, which we discussed in Chapter 2. It requires that politicians and bureaucrats in some jurisdictions devote time and resources to co-ordinating their policies with those of jurisdictions at other levels and in adjoining areas. In senior governments, this activity can become formalized and channelled through special intergovernmental affairs ministries. In smaller jurisdictions, external co-ordination can well become an activity engaged in by almost everyone in the government organization, regardless of the policy they administer: police, fire, hospital, schools, health, transportation, pollution, courts, tourism, industrial development, zoning, safety, and food inspection. Meetings, conferences, and liaison boards providing opportunities for negotiation and the sharing of information are the stuff of which co-ordination is made. The recent literature on 'trade in public goods'[11] provides examples of activities which demand the allocation to and use of resources for co-ordination activities.

11 A. Williams, 'The Optimal Provision of Public Goods in a System of Local Government,' *Journal of Political Economy* LXXIV 1 (February 1966) 18-33; M. Connolly, 'Trade in Public Goods: A Diagrammatic Analysis,' *Quarterly Journal of Economics* LXXVI 1 (February 1972) 61-78; and H.J. Kiesling, 'Public Goods and the Possibilities for Trade,' *Canadian Journal of Economics* VII 3 (August 1974) 402-17

4

The orthodox economic approach
to federalism

1 INTRODUCTION

The orthodox economic view of federalism or, as we have called it, of the structure of the public sector, rests on three basic assumptions: (*a*) that a structure exists, that is, that more than one jurisdictional level of government exists and therefore that the public sector can be described by something like the assignment table we have introduced in Chapter 3; (*b*) that public goods, externalities, or spill-overs and economies of scale such as those we described in Chapter 2 also exist; and (*c*) that organizational costs, ie, signalling, mobility, administration, and co-ordination costs, are zero. However, since these costs are usually not mentioned, this third assumption is generally implicit. In recent versions of the orthodox model,[1] one component of administration costs – the cost of setting up governments – has been made to be larger than zero and given a role to play.

We will argue[2] that assumptions (*a*) and (*c*) are inconsistent in that when organizational costs are zero it is not possible to make an assignment table determinate, that is, any outcome is possible. A table may degenerate to only one government, or to a single row, that is, to a single jurisdictional level with a large number of separate governments, or to other structures. We will further argue that the introduction of positive setting-up costs, though sufficient to limit the number of jurisdictions, cannot alone provide an explanation for multi-level, multi-unit public sector structures.

1 See G. Tullock, 'Federalism: Problems of Scale,' *Public Choice* VI (Spring 1969) 19-30; see also Wallace E. Oates, *Fiscal Federalism* (New York: Harcourt Brace Jovanovitch 1972) chapter 2.
2 In the summary and synthesis of the orthodox model which we present in this chapter we will often caricature the views of authors and neglect the nuances and subtleties of their arguments. To avoid being unfair, we make very few references to the literature.

We shall proceed as follows: first, we investigate what is meant by the statement that organizational costs are zero; then we summarize and extend the orthodox model; in Section 4, we introduce positive administration costs[3] and show how that affects the orthodox results; we argue that this new modified orthodox model is still unsatisfactory.

2 THE MEANING OF ZERO ORGANIZATIONAL COSTS

To assume that organizational costs to citizens and to governments are zero is equivalent to assuming that whoever (governments) makes decisions about the supply of public output and whoever (constituent assemblies) makes decisions about assigning functions to jurisdictional levels can acquire without cost correct information on preferences of all citizens and on the supply technologies for all outputs, that public bodies can be created and operated costlessly, and that all their activities can be co-ordinated also without costs.

Therefore, when organizational costs are zero, it is logically inconsistent to assume the existence of an institutional framework such as the one outlined in Chapter 3 (Section 7). Indeed, with organizational costs equal to zero, individuals will not be asked to register their preferences by voting, since these preferences are known or can be known without effort. Furthermore, no other decision rule can exist except unanimity. The entire notion of representative democracy is therefore superfluous and must be discarded.

The reader will have recognized that this is the stylized world of the theory of public goods. Indeed, it is from that theory that the orthodox view of federalism has been illegitimately developed. Sometimes, of course, some realism did creep in on an *ad hoc* basis, but essentially the currently accepted theory of the structure of the public sector is an application of the theory of public goods. And that is how it should be if organizational costs are zero, because, as we will show, in such a context it must follow that all utility functions and all production functions are known and that public goods are paid for by benefit taxes – or Lindahl prices.

3 THE SIMPLEST ORTHODOX VIEW

To emphasize our main point better, it will be useful if we summarize and extend what we take the dominant model to be. Consequently, we assume that each citizen *a* will maximize a well-behaved concave ordinal utility function defined for

3 One of the four components of organization costs

private and pure public goods.[4] Let X_h stand for the n private goods and S_k for the m public goods, then our assumption is formalized by saying that each a maximizes a function

$$U^a = U^a(X_h, S_k) \quad (a = 1, \dots, \ell) \tag{4.1}$$

for which $\partial U^a / \partial X_h$ and $\partial U^a / \partial S_k$ are assumed to be positive.[5] The prices that enter the constraint against which (4.1) is maximized are benefit tax rates or Lindhal prices.

These prices are defined as the rates of tax on a public good which, in relation to the price of a numéraire, are, for every person one by one, equal to the marginal rate of substitution of that public good for the numéraire or, as we will sometimes say for brevity, is equal to the marginal numéraire utility of the public good.

To make the theory of public goods applicable to the problem of the structure of the public sector, Samuelson's definition of public goods must be modified. This is easily done, since that definition is really open-ended. Indeed, recall that a pure public good is defined to be one 'which all enjoy in common ... '[6] Surely, a good need not be enjoyed – or available, as we prefer to put it – by everyone in the universe to be a public good. If a good is equally available to fifty individuals, we can say that it is a pure public good with a span of availability of fifty; another good which is equally available to 200,000 individuals is a pure public good with a span of 200,000, and so on for all public goods.

As indicated earlier, we do not consider the case of goods which are not equally available to all members of a group, but are not pure private goods; hence all public goods are pure public goods, even if the size of the group to which they

4 There is no doubt that the analysis would be more complex if we were to extend our argument to the case of non-private goods (goods 'which though not available equally to all, have the property that the amount available to one individual does not reduce that available to others by an equal amount' (A. Breton, 'A Theory of Government Grants,' *Canadian Journal of Economics and Political Science* XXXI 2 [May 1965] 177) and other heterogeneous or differentiated public goods. However, nothing would be gained in the present context by extending the model in that direction.

5 All public 'bads' can be transformed into public 'goods' simply by redefining the 'bad' into its negative. Hence garbage gives rise to garbage removal and pollution to pollution control and abatement. When Lindhal prices are charged, that transformation is sufficient to insure that the assumption of positive marginal utilities is meaningful, since these prices can be negative (subsidies). If Lindhal prices are not levied – contrary to our assumption – positive marginal utilities would require, in addition to the above transformation, that no public good which any one a dislikes ever be provided, if a contradiction is to be avoided.

6 P.A. Samuelson, 'The Pure Theory of Public Expenditure,' *Review of Economics and Statistics* XXVI 4 (November 1954) 387

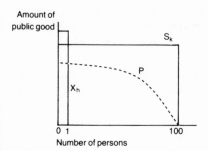

Figure 4.1

are equally available varies. It may help to clarify the nature of the definitions and of the assumptions made if we focus attention briefly on Figure 4.1. In that figure the vertical axis measures the amount or availability of public goods and the horizontal axis measures the number of persons to which goods are made available or the span of availability of the public goods. Three goods are portrayed in the figure. Good S_k (represented by the larger rectangular box) is provided equally to everyone in the group, but to no one outside that group, hence we will say that good S_k is a pure public good with a span of 100; good P (portrayed by the curve P) is also available to 100 individuals, but not in equal amounts, good P is thus a non-private good; and X_h (represented by the column or line X_h) is a pure private good. What we said above is that P type goods are not considered below.

We assume in what follows that all goods can be classified as rectangular boxes along a continuum such as the abscissa of Figure 4.1 beginning with pure private goods followed by such goods as pure club public goods, pure local public goods, pure metropolitan public goods, pure regional public goods, pure provincial public goods to pure national, world, and universal public goods. We are, of course, not asserting that such a classificatory system is a good representation of the variety of goods in the real world; indeed by ruling out non-private and other differentiated public goods we have implicitly recognized that the classification of all real world goods requires a more complex system. We use this one only because it is the prevailing one in the orthodox approach.

In such a world, let us assume that the constituent assembly chooses an assignment table Ω_0 for which the value of output (in terms of the pre-selected numéraire) is a maximum. Without asking how the constituent assembly got to Ω_0, what can be said about the properties of that assignment? Simply, that all functions are assigned to jurisdictional levels in such a way that externalities (or spillovers) are everywhere equal to zero. To put it differently, with Ω_0, interjurisdictional consumption externalities are all equal to zero, as a result of the fact that the constituent assembly has assigned national goods to a national jurisdictional level, regional goods to a regional level, metropolitan goods to a metropolitan level, club goods to a club level, etc. and that benefit taxes are levied to pay for them. This arrangement has already been described as a 'perfect mapping' of functions into jurisdictional levels[7]; the term 'fiscal equivalence'[8] and more recently that of 'perfect correspondence' of functions and jurisdictional levels[9] have also been used more or less for the same purpose; in the present context we say that it depicts a 'perfect assignment table.'

The orthodox way of visualizing the assignment table is to recognize that, for every club good, local good, regional good, etc., there is a corresponding jurisdiction (not jurisdictional level, the existence of which is generally not recognized). To illustrate, begin by considering an assignment that is not perfect, such as the one portrayed in Figure 4.2. In that figure, the ordinate measures the equilibrium

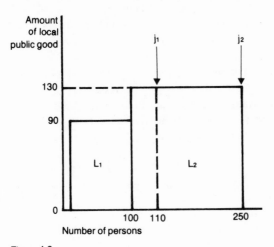

Figure 4.2

supply of and demand for one local public good, L, which, we assume, is provided in amounts of $L_1 = 90$ and $L_2 = 130$ units by jurisdictions j_1 and j_2 respectively; the abscissa measures both the span of public goods and the number of persons

7 Breton, 'A Theory of Government Grants' 180
8 M. Olson, Jr, 'The Principle of "Fiscal Equivalence": The Division of Responsibilities among Different Levels of Government,' *American Economic Review* LIX 2 (May 1969) 483
9 Oates, *Fiscal Federalism* 33. The concept of jurisdictional levels was not clearly distinguished from that of jurisdictions in the contributions of such writers as Breton, Olson, and Oates.

per jurisdiction. L_1 has a span of 100 and L_2 one of 150 persons, while j_1 contains 110 individuals and j_2 140. As is clear from the diagram, if the government of j_2 supplies any positive amount L_2 of L some of it would spill over into j_1 (to individuals 101 to 110). The value of this spill-over could only be ascertained by knowing the exact amount of L_2 supplied and the utility functions of persons 101 to 110 in j_1. The perfect assignment table is one from which the spill-over portrayed in Figure 4.2 has been eliminated.

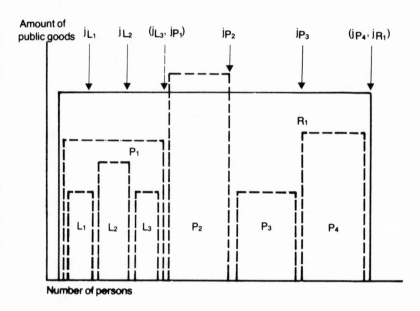

Figure 4.3

A less simple assignment table admits a larger number of public goods and jurisdictions. In Figure 4.3, L_1, L_2 and L_3 refer to a local good, P_1, P_2, P_3, and P_4 to a provincial good, R_1 to a regional good, and the j's depict the boundaries of local, provincial, and regional jurisdictions. As Figure 4.3 is drawn, there are no spillovers and it therefore depicts a perfect assignment table: one in which every kind of public good has its own jurisdiction.

Before we describe in more detail the properties of the perfect assignment table, we note that it is defined without any specific reference to the production of public goods and services. To see that this is how it should be, note that to achieve the largest possible numéraire value of output the constituent assembly cannot have a preference for any particular jurisdictional location of any production activities. Such activities will instead be spatially located strictly in such a way as to minimize production and transportation costs. It need not consider the particular assignment of functions entrenched in the perfect assignment table Ω_0.

To examine this result in more detail, consider the case of a public good produced subject to long-run (technological) economies of scale and assume that the good is a local one whose span of availability is therefore 'small'; assume also that the function or power to supply that particular good has been assigned to 'many' different local jurisdictions. The constituent assembly will not be dismayed by such a situation. It will simply insure that production is centralized so as to yield the economies of larger scale and it will see to it that consumption is 'decentralized' according to the dictates of the perfect assignment table.

That table will therefore display the following properties: for every public good produced under increasing or over-all constant marginal cost conditions, the number and size of jurisdictions and the assignment of functions to these jurisdictions will be such that the marginal rates of substitution of the public good for the numéraire summed over all individuals in each jurisdiction will equal its marginal numéraire costs of production. If there are goods produced under decreasing marginal cost conditions, that is, goods which still display exploitable economies of scale after demand has everywhere been met, then the equilibrium conditions will be different for every good in the economy whether public or private, since when marginal costs are decreasing average costs exceed them and subsidies (and hence, taxes) are necessary for maximum social output.

It will be easier to examine that case if we turn to the implicit 'price side' of the perfect assignment table and make use of the assumption that public goods are paid for by benefit taxes levied at constant marginal rates over varying output levels. This will also help to clarify the nature of the assignment problem in this model and some as yet unexplored features of the perfect assignment table.

If *some* of the production processes in the economy, whether of private or of public goods, are characterized by decreasing marginal costs, a perfect assignment table will require that the sum of the marginal prices for each and every public good and the individual prices of private goods should deviate from their respective marginal costs by an amount which is inversely proportional to the elasticity of demand for the goods.[10] The demand in question is, for public goods, the vertical sum over citizens of their respective demand curves, while, for private goods, it is the horizontal sum over quantities of the individual demand curves.

The reader will surely have noted one striking aspect of this solution to the assignment problem, namely that it is identically the same as the solution to the

10 W.J. Baumol and D.F. Bradford, 'Optimal Departures from Marginal Cost Pricing,'
   American Economic Review LX 3 (June 1970) 265-83

problem of the allocation of scarce resources in a unitary state governed by a benevolent dictator or planner. To put it differently, under the assumptions of the theory of public goods extended to include goods of different spans, the solution to the assignment problem is the solution to the problem of allocation of scarce resources, so much so that it is possible to say that there is no assignment problem at all.[11] Indeed, in this model the concepts of assignment table and of jurisdictions are superfluous; we used them only to summarize the orthodox theory and to make a point. In particular, with respect to the notion of jurisdictions, it should be noted that the assumption that organizational resource costs are zero implies that the solution to the assignment problem is indeterminate or more exactly meaningless. Indeed with that assumption there can be as many jurisdictions as there are public goods, only one jurisdiction, no jurisdiction at all, or any arbitrary intermediate number. A simple result, but one which appears to have been quite often missed.

We conclude that, in a world of zero organizational costs, the search for a theory of the structure of the public sector or of federalism is fruitless. The basic question of such a theory – that of the assignment of functions – does not even arise! This is not a trivial point; from it we derive the notion that the essential nature of a structure for the public sector is to be found in the presence of positive organizational resource costs, not in public goods or externalities.

4 POSITIVE ADMINISTRATION COSTS

Let us now assume that decisions about public output are made and implemented by bodies that use up personnel, equipment, and other resources. These bodies are not the public bodies or governments that we observe in the real world, however, since they are still assumed to know all individual preferences because signalling and mobility costs are zero. Therefore these governments charge benefit taxes to pay for the public goods they supply. The only difference from the model of the previous section is the assumption that bodies exist which engage in costly administrative activities. In other words, resources are needed for administration, but not for any other organizational activities and therefore not for co-ordination, signalling, or mobility.

Given this context, let us assume as we did in the previous section that the

11 This point was, to our knowledge, first recognized by J.C. Weldon ['Public Goods (and Federalism)' *Canadian Journal of Economics and Political Science* XXXII 2 (May 1966) 231], who correctly argued against Breton that under the conditions postulated a 'perfect mapping is complete centralization, while in a general sense it is the creation of a single government for any group that chooses to have or is given a specified social welfare function.'

constituent assembly chooses an assignment table Ω_0' for which the numéraire value of output is a maximum. As in the model of the last section, the value of output is maximized when externalities are minimized. In the present context, however, the presence of resource-using bodies implies that the minimum will only be zero when interjurisdictional grants or payments of a special sort (to be discussed below) exist.

To understand the nature of the optimum, we must recognize that since governments are costly to set up and to operate, the constituent assembly will only create them up to the point where the marginal potential gains in utility from a reduction in externalities are equal to the marginal real resource costs of forming more or larger jurisdictions and hence of setting up and operating more or larger public bodies. It will clarify the meaning of this first-order equilibrium condition to consider a situation where only one jurisdictional level exists and focus on how things look at the boundary between only two jurisdictions.

Imagine, therefore, that we are considering the jurisdictional level to which pure local public goods have been assigned. Assume for simplicity that all local goods have the same span of 100. Assume further, given the production conditions and the utility functions of the relevant group of citizens, that when the jurisdiction encompasses 265 citizens the marginal administration cost of the institution supplying the public goods in that jurisdiction is exactly equal to the marginal welfare or dead weight loss from the externality that must then obtain. The picture in that jurisdiction would look as follows. Some 'first' one hundred individuals – somehow identified – could want, let us say, 75 units of the public good and the government will supply them with 75 units and charge each one of them a tax price equal to the marginal value each individual places on the pure local public good. If a 'second' group of 100 individuals wants 200 units of the public good it would be treated in like fashion. Suppose that a 'third' group of individuals exists and that if it was completely located in the jurisdiction, would want, let us say, 150 units of the public good, but since only 65 individuals of that group are in the jurisdiction (the other 35 are in another jurisdiction), only 60 units are desired and supplied, and financed by the use of benefit tax prices. In equilibrium and before any interjurisdictional grants, therefore, externalities exist whose value is derived from the utility functions of individuals within the span of the good, but outside the boundary of the jurisdiction.

We can represent the above result diagrammatically as in Figure 4.4, where on the horizontal axis we again measure the number of persons and on the vertical axis we indicate the amount of the local public good. The argument above states that individuals 201 to 265 are provided with 60 units of the good and pay a tax price which reflects the marginal value of the good to them. Individuals 266 to 300 are also provided with 60 units, but do not pay for what they get. The situa-

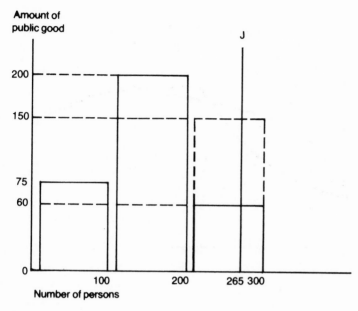

Figure 4.4

tion is consequently not a Pareto-optimal one. To achieve optimality, interjurisdictional grants will have to be introduced.

These will be unusual grants, since in effect they will be 'conditional benefit
grants' paid to individuals 201 to 265 and levied in the form of benefit taxes on
individuals 266 to 300, not on all individuals in that jurisdiction. To put it differently, grants or subsidies will have to be paid to 65 individuals in the jurisdiction – the 65 whose own utility functions give rise to a demand for 60 units of
the public good – and a corresponding tax levied on only 35 individuals in the
'other' jurisdiction – the 35 who fall in the span of the local public good and
whose own demand added to that of the first 65 generates a total demand for
150 units of the public good. All taxes and grants have to be Lindahl taxes and
Lindahl grants.

We must now inquire not only into the properties of the system at the boundary between each pair of jurisdictions as we have done, but also ask how many
jurisdictions will be observed in equilibrium at each jurisdictional level. Such an
analysis can be conducted with the help of Figure 4.5. On the ordinate of that
figure, we measure the total gains, G, to the citizens of the 'federation' from a
reduction in externalities that results from changing the number of jurisdictions
and the total costs, C, of administering institutions in these jurisdictions.

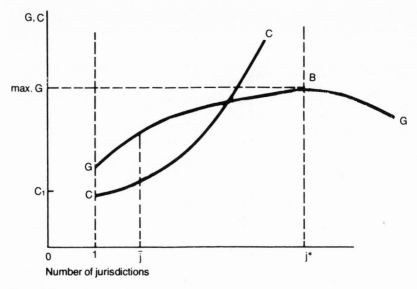

Figure 4.5

To ascertain what the characteristics of the G and C curves are, consider the situation when only one jurisdiction exists. At that point the total gains from the existence of the institution are at least no smaller than its costs; otherwise jurisdictions themselves would not exist. If total gains are exactly equal to total costs, the equilibrium (optimal) number of jurisdictions is one, a situation which implies that all individuals have identical homothetic utility functions (so that redistribution of incomes does not alter the demand for public goods) or that all goods have the same span – assumptions that appear unreasonable at least for the world taken as a whole and that are certainly inconsistent with the assumptions of the model. We conclude, therefore, that the G curve must lie above the C curve at the point where the number of jurisdictions is one.

In addition, we know that there exists a number of jurisdictions j^* for which the additional gains from reductions in externalities are zero: this number is equal to the number of jurisdictions which eliminate all externalities; it was derived in the last section and is equal to the number of jurisdictions that results from setting administration costs equal to zero. That number, labelled B in Figure 4.5, must be above and to the right of point C_1 on the C curve. It is the highest point on the G curve, since increases in the number of jurisdictions must lead to over-internalization of externalities and to reductions in gains. If we made strong assumptions about individual utility functions and their aggregation (assumptions that we examine briefly below) we could also show that the G curve is not scalloped – that it is as we have drawn it. In general, however, it will be scalloped, though having to go through point B it will on the whole fall forward.

On the cost side, the most reasonable assumptions lead to the view that the C curve will depict increasing or constant cost of administering new institutions. If we so assume, it is easy to read the optimal number of jurisdictions directly from the G and C curves in the diagram. In Figure 4.5 it is $\bar{j}$. At that number of jurisdictions the net value of output in that society is a maximum. At $\bar{j}$ also, we know that there remains flows of externalities that are not internalized because the real marginal costs are larger than the real marginal gains of doing so.

If, however, the marginal administration costs of new jurisdictions were decreasing, the equilibrium number of jurisdictions could lie to the right of j^*. In a world in which only administration costs exist, it is quite conceivable that amalgamation of two jurisdictions, for example, two municipalities, will more than double administration costs.

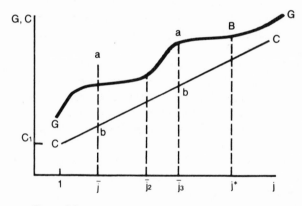

Figure 4.6

If the given G curve displays a pattern like the one illustrated in Figure 4.6 – a possibility that cannot be ruled out – the constituent assembly will have to call upon total conditions in addition to marginal ones to discriminate between points $\bar{j}_1$ or $\bar{j}_3$ – note that $(a - b) = (a' - b')$ – and j_2, but it will not be able to distinguish between j_1 and j_3 – certainly not by using total and marginal conditions, since they are identical in the two cases – so that the possibility exists that a large and a small number of jurisdictions may both be optimal at the same time.

Let us look into this result more carefully and examine why the possibility of multiple equilibria exists. The first thing to observe is that multiple equilibria are the product of the fact that the G curve is scalloped. The G curve, it will be re-called, is a relationship describing the increase in the aggregate welfare of the citizens of a country as the number of jurisdictions is increased and hence as the value of the flow of externalities is reduced. What the scalloped segments of the curve describe are 'inadvertent' changes in the distribution of real (utility) incomes brought about by changes in the number of jurisdictions. To put it differently, as the number of jurisdictions is continuously increased the changes that are brought about in the amount of externalities need not always be in the direction of reducing them. This is because there are no reasons why successive changes in jurisdictional boundaries should affect individuals in any particular ordering of the intensity of their preferences. Indeed, if changes in jurisdictional boundaries (or if the creation of new jurisdictions) bring some individuals with lower intensity of preferences in equilibrium before some individuals with higher intensity, then the G curve will be scalloped as in Figure 4.6.[12]

What will be the ultimate equilibrum point? Or to put it differently, which of j_1 or j_3 is the 'best' number of jurisdictions? The answer depends on the policy of 'purposive' income redistribution that is pursued, since the only real welfare difference between j_1 and j_3 is the distribution of real income. This is not a problem that we examine here.

The introduction of positive administration costs – other organizational costs being held at zero – appears to have provided us with a 'public sector structure' in which the number of jurisdictions will be different from and probably less than the number of different public goods with different spans. Either way, greater or smaller, the likelihood is that a given jurisdiction will provide more than one public good. If that is the case it is an important step.

However, the reader will have recognized that this analysis is not really very different from that of the simple orthodox model. Both begin with the postulate that a structure (more than one jurisdiction) must exist.

The modified orthodox model of this section determines the number of jurisdictions by appealing to administration costs. Would such costs really give rise to a public sector with a structure in a world in which signalling and mobility costs

12 The foregoing argument is not dissimilar to the one related to intersecting community indifference curves. See, for example, T. Scitovsky, 'A Reconsideration of the Theory of Tariff,' in American Economic Association, *Readings in the Theory of International Trade* (Philadelphia: Blakiston Co. 1949) 358-67; see also P.A. Samuelson, 'Social Indifference Curves,' *Quarterly Journal of Economics* LXX 1 (February 1956) 1-22, reprinted in J.E. Stiglitz, ed., *The Collected Scientific Papers of P.A. Samuelson* (Cambridge MA: MIT Press 1966) Chapter 78.

were zero, and in which, therefore, preferences were known and Lindahl prices consequently feasible? The answer is no, because in such circumstances the task of providing public policies could always be performed by one government only. It follows that the constructions of Figures 4.5 and 4.6 under these conditions degenerate to $j = 1$, or are indeterminate.

It is only when we drop the idea that utility functions are known and that benefit taxes are levied, but still hold to the notion that public goods generating spill-overs and externalities exist and that production processes with economies of scale that cannot be exploited costlessly also exist, that the full package of organizational costs appears and provides us with a rationale for a public sector structure. To put it differently, it is to economize on these costs that structures exist in the public sector, just as it is to economize on transaction and search costs that money exists[13] and to economize on monitoring and enforcement costs that firms and other similar institutions exist.[14]

13 M. Perlman, 'The Roles of Money in an Economy and the Optimum Quantity of Money,' *Economica*, NS, XXXVIII 151 (August 1971) 233-54

14 R.H. Coase, 'The Nature of the Firm,' in American Economic Association, *Readings in Price Theory* (Homewood: Richard D. Irwin, Inc. 1952) 331-51; A.A. Alchian and H. Demsetz, 'Production, Information Costs, and Economic Organization,' *American Economic Review* LXII 5 (December 1972) 777-95; J. McManus, 'The Organization of Production (unpublished PHD dissertation, University of Toronto 1971)

PART TWO
MODELS OF FEDERALISM

5

Citizens and governments

Three different kinds of actors are needed to articulate and resolve the models of Chapters 7 and 8: citizens, politicians, and bureaucrats. When we focus on decisions pertaining to the formulation and implementation of *policies*, politicians and bureaucrats are said to be engaged in a governmental role and the institutions they are deemed to constitute are called governments. When they are concerned with the assignment of *functions*, politicians and bureaucrats are deemed to be performing a constitutional role and the institutions which they are then conceived to be operating we call constituent assemblies.

In this chapter, after a discussion of the hypothesis governing the behaviour of citizens, we examine the behaviour of politicians – and more superficially that of bureaucrats – in their governmental role. In the next chapter we analyse their roles as members of constituent assemblies.

More specifically, we suggested in Chapter 3 that citizens participate in the political process by investing time and money in two general types of activities which we called signalling and mobility. We also suggested that governments invest in administration and in co-ordination. In the next section, we seek to provide a rationale for these investments by citizens, and in Sections 3 and 4 we seek to accomplish the same thing for governments.

In both Sections 2 and 3, we pay particular attention to the variations in the flow of resources that are allocated by citizens and governments to signalling, mobility, administration, and co-ordination as the degree of centralization is changed, that is, as functions are reassigned between jurisdictional levels, or to put it still differently, as the assignment table is changed and the structure of the public sector correspondingly altered.

2 THE ADJUSTMENT OF CITIZENS

Why do citizens invest some of their scarce resources to signal their preferences to governments and / or to move to other jurisdictions? To put it in its simplest form, because they estimate that such investments will have a yield or return per unit of resources invested that will be at least as high as resources invested in alternative opportunities. We must therefore inquire into the nature and properties of the yield expected by citizens from the opportunities to invest in signalling and mobility.

The degree of coercion or frustration

One approach that has often been adopted[1] consists in assuming that every citizen can be represented by a well-behaved, concave ordinal utility function defined over public, non-private, and private goods. It is then assumed that citizens maximize such a function subject to a budget constraint defined for private goods that are purchased (or sold) at market prices, and for non-private and public goods which are assumed to be made available or supplied at given tax or pseudo prices. Equilibrium with respect to private goods is reached by the purchase (or sale) of these goods by citizens at the ruling market prices. However, since non-private and public goods are not purchased nor sold by citizens acting individually, the general outcome with respect to these goods is one that, in general, results in a disequilibrium.

Since the loss in utility that obtains in disequilibrium can be measured – and if the marginal utility of money is assumed constant it can be given a monetary dimention – the magnitude has sometimes been given a name. In *The Economic Theory of Representative Government*, Breton called it 'coercion.'

Reduction in the degree of coercion is the return that citizens can expect from engaging in mobility or in signalling activities. To put it differently, the increment in utility that results from having a government alter the provision of public or non-private goods, or the tax prices levied to pay for these goods consequent on signalling by citizens, or the improvement in welfare following a move to a more congenial jurisdiction is the return on investing in organizational activities by citizens.

1 G. Tullock, 'Social Cost and Government Action,' *American Economic Review* LIX 2 (May 1969) 189-97; Y. Barzel, 'Two Propositions on the Optimum Level of Producing Collective Goods,' *Public Choice* VI (Spring 1969) 31-7; J.M. Buchanan, 'Notes for an Economic Theory of Socialism,' *Public Choice* (Spring 1970); Wallace E. Oates, *Fiscal Federalism* (New York: Harcourt Brace Jovanovich 1972) Chapter 2 and appendix; and A. Breton, *The Economic Theory of Representative Government* (Chicago: Aldine 1974) Chapter 4

Though this rationale to an understanding of the nature of the yield on signalling and mobility can serve some purpose, it must be recognized that the assumption basic to it – that citizens face given tax or pseudo prices – is a very restrictive one. It has two parts: first, it states that the marginal price of any non-private or public good (or policy) is equal to its average price over the 'relevant' quantities and / or qualities; and second, though not least important, it states that citizens are able to impute to each non-private and public good provided to them a particular portion of the sum total of the money that each pays to governments in the form of income, sales, property, excise, customs, and other taxes. Because this assumption is so restrictive we have decided to suggest a different rationale for coercion which does seem, to us at least, to be more realistic.

To do this, we still assume that each citizen can be represented by a well-behaved, concave, ordinal utility function, but to simplify, we also assume that the utility function is weakly separable in that private goods can be partitioned into one group and non-private and public goods into another. This form of the utility function allows us to recognize, initially at least, that is, before any signalling or moving takes place, that citizens do not control the amount (and / or quality) of public policies supplied to them – and only very indirectly[2] the total amount of taxes they pay.

We then assume that each citizen adds up the benefits – measured in utility units or in dollar equivalents – derived from each public policy supplied by a particular government; and, that in a similar way, the costs – again in utility units or in dollars – of taxes and other payments made to that government, that is, of private goods foregone, are also added up.

If we impute a given time horizon to each citizen, it is possible to assume that each calculates the present value of benefits and costs – in similar units of measurement – by using some rate of discount. The difference between the two discounted streams is the contribution of the policies of a governmental unit j to citizen a's net worth. To be specific, if we let B_t^{aj} be the benefits evaluated by a to accrue to him at time t from government j, C_t^{aj} be the costs evaluated in a similar fashion, d^a be the rate of discount used by a, then over the time horizon T, the net worth from governmental unit j accruing to a will be.

$$W^{aj} = \Sigma_{t=T}^{T} [B_t^{aj} / (1 + d^a)^t] - [C_t^{aj} / (1 + d^a)^t] \tag{5.1}$$

From (5.1) it is easy to calculate changes in net worth that would result from

2 Because citizens have some control over their purchases of goods and services, the amount of labour supplied, etc., they have some control over the exact amount they pay in taxes to governments, but that is surely only a minimal and indirect degree of control.

changes in government policies. It is true, of course that the benefits and / or costs of those policies which affect a citizen only indirectly may be difficult to evaluate and therefore their contribution to a citizen's net worth or to changes therein may be uncertain, but, for the purpose at hand, we can assume that citizens are able to calculate W^{aj}.

We should emphasize before we move any further ahead that it is possible for (5.1) to be negative as well as positive. In other words, it is possible for a government to impose more costs on an individual than it confers benefits on him.

We then make the following additional assumption: whenever a public policy is implemented by governmental unit j, it will increase the degree of coercion or frustration borne by a if the change in W^{aj} is negative. Specifically, we assume that if

$$d \mid W^{aj} \mid < 0 \tag{5.2}$$

then

$$d \, \phi_T > 0 \tag{5.3}$$

where ϕ_T is a measure of coercion or frustration at time τ.

Using (5.3), it is a simple matter to arrive at a measure of a total amount of coercion borne by a given citizen at a moment in time.

The amount of resources invested in political participation
Citizens invest time and money in political participation, that is in moving and signalling, because the use of resources in these activities reduces the amount of frustration they have to endure. To put it differently, we can say that the gross yield on investment in political participation is the increase in net worth derived from the consumption of public policies.

To give formal representation to the idea of the last paragraph, let us measure coercion in money units. We can then calculate the present value of the stream of frustration which obtains in the absence of political participation at the beginning of $t = 1$. That sum is equal to

$$V_{\phi^a} = \Sigma_{t=1}^{T} [\phi_t^a / (1 + \rho^a)^t] \tag{5.4}$$

where T is again the length of the time horizon and ρ is a discount factor whose precise meaning will be defined shortly.

Now assume that all of a particular investment of time and money in political participation takes place just at the beginning of the first period $t = 1$; assume further that the reduced frustration that results from the investment obtaining in each time period is equal to ϕ_t^a and has a present value equal to

$$V_{\phi^a} = \Sigma_{t=1}^T \left[(\phi_t^a \,/\, (1 + \rho^a)^t \right]. \tag{5.5}$$

The particular rate of discount ρ^a that makes $V_{\phi^a} = V_{\hat\phi^a}$ is the yield or internal rate of return on investment in political participation by citizen a. In equilibrium, and assuming perfect capital markets,[3] our typical citizen will invest in political participation up to the point where the internal rate of return to him is equal to the given real market rate of interest, that is up to $\rho^a = i$. Specifically, if we let H_Z be investment in political participation, then when $\rho^a = i$ the amount of capital invested in political participation by citizen a is:

$$H_Z^* = \Sigma_{t=1}^T \left[(\phi^a - \hat\phi^a)_t \,/\, (1 + i)^t \right]. \tag{5.6}$$

That amount is equal to H_μ^* invested in mobility plus H_σ^* invested in signalling.[4] These equilibrium statements are, of course, valid on the usual assumption that as i falls, the amount of investment increases.

More on investment in political participation

The foregoing discussion was based on a partial specification of the investment in political participation function relating investment in political participation to its internal rate of return. We wish now to augment that function to include the centralization co-efficient and thus be in a position to examine how the amount of resources invested in political participation varies when γ varies. We therefore write

$$H_Z^a = H_Z^a(\rho_Z^a, \gamma) \quad (a = 1, \ldots, \ell) \tag{5.7}$$

where as before Z is political participation. It should be stressed that (5.7) is still a partial specification of the investment function, being limited to only those variables which are of interest to us now. Other variables are introduced in Chapter 7.

In discussing investment behaviour by citizens, we will usually divide political participation into its component parts, since the marginals of investment in the components as γ is altered may not have the same sign. We therefore write

$$H_\mu^a = H_\mu^a(\rho_\mu^a, \gamma) \quad (a = 1, \ldots, \ell) \tag{5.8}$$

and

$$H_\sigma^a = H_\sigma^a(\rho_\sigma^a, \gamma) \quad (a = 1, \ldots, \ell) \tag{5.9}$$

where μ and σ represent mobility and signalling respectively.

3 Some aspects of abandoning this assumption are discussed in Chapter 7.
4 Since this is not our main task, we will not pause to suggest empirical tests of how the amount of capital invested in political participation varies with changes in the rate of

As will become clear in Chapter 7, to determine an equilibrium centralization co-efficient we need some assumptions about the signs of the partial derivative of (5.8) and (5.9) with respect to γ. As will also become clear, an equilibrium can be determined on different assumptions about the sign of these two derivatives, or to state it in alternative fashion, on different assumptions about the extent to which political participation by citizens varies as γ varies. However, the assumptions we choose to make about these derivatives have to be consistent with other assumptions that will be needed below. In anticipation of this as well as to give more substance to the discussion that follows and to relate our own construction to previous efforts in this area of research, we assume and seek to justify that

$$H^{a'}_{\mu\gamma} < 0 \tag{5.10'}$$

and that

$$H^{a'}_{\sigma\gamma} \lesseqgtr 0 \tag{5.11''}$$

or summing over all citizens $C\ (= \Sigma^l_1 a)$ we assume that

$$H^{C'}_{\mu\gamma} < 0 \tag{5.10}$$

and that

$$H^{C'}_{\sigma\gamma} \lesseqgtr 0 \tag{5.11'}$$

where

$$H^{a'}_{\mu\gamma} = \partial H^a_\mu / \partial \gamma, \text{ etc.}$$

To justify these assumptions, we may, referring to the views of such students of the structure of the public sector as Stigler, Pennock, and Oates,[5] adopt the assumption that as γ increases, that is, as the degree of centralization increases, the variance of the distribution of the preferences of citizens within each jurisdiction increases, while that between jurisdictions falls. This process is relatively easy to visualize in the following very simple case, taken from Pennock's discussion. Suppose that in a society made up of 100 citizens, 60 favour a given policy, while 40

interest, with changes in income, and with changes in age, that is, how it varies over the life cycle of the individual. For partial equilibrium discussions that relate political participation to the interest rate see A.D. Scott, 'Investing and Protesting,' *Journal of Political Economy* LXXVII 6 (November-December 1969) 916-20, and A. Breton, 'Student Unrest and the Yield on Human Capital,' *Canadian Journal of Economics* VII 3 (August 1974) 434-8.
5 G.J. Stigler, 'The Tenable Range of Functions of Local Government,' Joint Economic Committee, *Federal Expenditure Policy for Economic Growth and Stability* (Washington, DC: Government Printing Office 1957) 213-19; J.R. Pennock, 'Federal and Unitary Government: Disharmony and Frustration,' *Behavioral Science* IV 2 (April 1959) 149-57; and Oates, *Fiscal Federalism* 54-63

oppose it and favour another. With simple majority, the policy implemented will be the one supported by 60 per cent of the citizens. Call that policy S_1. Suppose that instead of one jurisdiction, the society is broken in two equal size jurisdictions. In one of these, let us say j_1, 30 citizens favour S_2 (the other policy) and 20 support S_1. Since the size of the population is unchanged, in the other jurisdiction j_2, 40 citizens must want S_1 and the 10 remaining citizens must favour S_2. In j_2, policy S_1 will be implemented and in j_1 it will be S_2. Whereas with a unitary structure the preferences of 40 per cent of the citizens are not met, in the 'decentralized' structure that number falls to 30 per cent. This result will always obtain when there are only two policies and when the division of jurisdiction does not split the minority evenly. (Even when divided evenly, the minority is not worse off.)

If the assumption is accepted, it is possible to provide a rationale of some kind for (5.10) and (5.11′). Let us begin with the first. When the variance in the distribution of preferences between jurisdictions is large, that is when γ is low, an increase in that co-efficient will make it more difficult for any citizen who is seeking a location that will provide him with the bundle of public policies that he favours to find such a location, so that the amount of resources he will profitably invest in mobility will be smaller than when the possibility of finding a desirable location is large. At the limit when $\gamma = 1$, that is when all functions are assigned to one unique government, it will not be profitable – nor in that limiting case possible – for anyone to move from one jurisdiction to another. To put it differently, the yield on resources invested in mobility falls as γ rises and, given the market rate of interest, the amount of resources invested in that political activity also falls.

The indeterminate nature of (5.11′) may be justified as follows. Recall that signalling is defined to include such activities as searching for the preferences of other citizens in the jurisdiction, convincing them of a given point of view and organizing them so that a common front can be presented to the elected representatives. On the one hand, it seems reasonable to suppose that when γ is high, that is, when the variance of the distribution of the preferences of citizens within jurisdictions is small, the yield on \$1.00 invested in these activities is low and consequently less resources will be invested in signalling than when γ is low. On the other hand, the reduction in the level of frustration that can be achieved when γ is high may be so much greater than when γ is low, that the yield on investment in signalling increases with increases in γ, and consequently that more resources will be invested than when γ is low. For the sake of conducting the analysis below, we will assume that the relative weights of these two opposite forces are such that

$$H^{C'}_{\sigma\gamma} > 0. \tag{5.11}$$

The reader should keep in mind, however, that even if the exact equilibrium level of γ that is obtained depends on the specific assumptions made, the model can accommodate other assumptions with respect to (5.10) and (5.11). The facts will have to dictate the most relevant assumptions to make. In the absence of facts, consistency with other assumptions will be our only guide.

The effect of the behaviour of other citizens
So far we have analysed the behaviour of a typical citizen in isolation; to be more specific we have assumed that investment in mobility and / or in signalling undertaken by other citizens has no influence on citizen a's own investment behaviour.

We must relax this assumption. The effect of the migration of other citizens and of their signalling on the investment behaviour of citizen a will depend on how that migration and signalling will affect the degree of frustration endured by a. That in turn will depend on how migration and signalling affects a's benefits from, and costs of, public policies.

If citizen a expects the (inward or outward) migration of other citizens and / or their signalling to succeed in altering public policies in a way that he deems adverse to himself, and consequently to reduce the value of the net worth he derives from the public policies, he may decide himself to invest in mobility and / or signalling to counter these effects, even if the amount of coercion to which he is directly subjected would not otherwise have induced him to invest. We conclude that investment in political participation by a is a function not only of coercion but also of expected coercion.

3 THE BEHAVIOUR OF GOVERNMENTS

Whereas it seemed reasonable to assume that citizens dispose of their resources in such a way as to maximize their utility, the real problem confronting anyone who wishes to analyse the behaviour of governments is that of deciding on the most appropriate objective function to impute to these institutions.

Governments operate within the context of the institutional framework described in Chapter 3, and in that context the objective function that makes most sense is that of a utility function defined over a probability of re-election variable and some other variables such as honour, statesmanship, place in history, and private wealth. Or alternatively, but equivalently, one could say that politicians in office (or governing parties) maximize a utility function, defined for public policies, subject to the constraint of a probability of re-election function, and to an additional constraint which states that the probability of re-election variable should not fall below some critical value if the governing party is to be re-elected. In this second form, the problem is that of maximizing the utility functions

$$U^p = U^p (S_k, e_i) \quad (k = 1, \dots m; \ i = 1, \dots n) \tag{5.12}$$

subject to the production functions

$$S_k = S_k(L_k, K_k), \quad (k = 1, \dots m) \tag{5.13}$$

to the re-election function

$$\pi^p = \pi^p(S_k, e_i, c) \quad (k = 1, \dots m; \; i = 1, \dots n) \tag{5.14}$$

and to

$$\pi^p \geq \pi^{p^*} \tag{5.15}$$

where S_k are public policies, e_i stand for honour, statemanship, place in history, private wealth, etc., π^p is the probability of re-election variable, L_k and K_k are labour and capital, π^{p^*} is the critical value of π^p that must be achieved if the governing party is to be re-elected, and c is the degree of competition between parties in the public sector.

The maximization is not an easy one to resolve, and indeed in its above general form has no determinate solution.[6] However, that form helps us to understand that governments preoccupied by the probability of their re-election can supply output produced and / or procured at minimum cost as is implicit in (5.13).

We will therefore assume in the remainder of this study that in producing and / or purchasing public goods for citizens governments seek to minimize costs;[7] furthermore, we hold to the view that this assumption is not inconsistent with the maximization of a utility function defined for the probability of re-election or for one defined for public goods and constrained by equations (5.14) and (5.15).

We assume that in addition to the usual labour and capital (inventories, machines, or structures) which governments need to produce or acquire public policies, they invest resources (time and money) in two special types of capital which we have called administration and co-ordination. The reader will recall from the discussion of Chapter 3 that administration includes the search by politicians for information about the preferences of citizens; it comprises the activities surrounding the formulation of, and decisions related to, supply, regulation, income redistribution, and other policies, as well as the implementation and enforcement of these policies and the activities required to induce citizens to comply with laws. It also includes the setting up and the operation of governmental units, defined to comprise, in this case, subsidiary bodies such as agencies and Crown

---

6 The main reason for that conclusion is that (5.14) is not a simple relationship, but is one for which increases in some S_k's lead to increases in π^p when certain citizens are considered and to decreases when other citizens are the object of attention. For an analysis of these problems, see Breton, *Economic Theory of Representative Government*.

7 This assumption is less restrictive than it may seem in that it is consistent with a supply of public policies in excess of the amount that is socially optimal.

corporations. The reader will also recall that co-ordination refers to activities involving a number of governments and governmental agencies that are required for the purpose of dealing with spill-overs, exploitable economies of scale, and other interactions and interdependencies.

What amount of resources will governments, taken one by one, invest in these two kinds of activities? As was the case with citizens, the answer is that investment in administration and in co-ordination will be undertaken as long as the internal rate of return on these investments exceeds the market rate of interest. The internal rate of return is, again as in the previous section, the rate which equalizes the present value of the stream of utility to governing parties[8] from public policies when no investments are undertaken with the stream when some are made.

In equilibrium, the amount invested in administration by all governments will be H_A^{G*} and the amount invested in co-ordination will be H_E^{G*}. We must now ask how these two magnitudes will vary as γ, the centralization co-efficient, varies. As with political participation by citizens, our model can accommodate alternative assumptions concerning the signs of the partial derivatives of investment in co-ordination and administration with respect to γ. However, as we will emphasize in Chapter 7, these assumptions have to be consistent with those we have made about the adjustment of citizens if our model is to have a stable solution. For this reason and also for the sake of concreteness, we assume and seek to justify that

$$H_{E\gamma}^{G'} < 0 \qquad (5.16)$$

and that

$$H_{A\gamma}^{G'} \geq 0 \qquad (5.17')$$

where

$$H_{E\gamma}^{G'} = H_E^G / \partial\gamma, \text{ etc.}$$

Providing a rationale for (5.16) is relatively simple. As the number of jurisdictions falls and as their spatial dimension consequently increases, the extent and magnitude of interjurisdictional spill-overs, economies of scale, and externalities, or as we have called them interactions and interdependencies, are reduced and less investment in co-ordination is required to obtain a given result.

We assume (5.17') to be positive or zero, because as γ increases, the reduction in investment to set up and operate governmental units may be offset by the increased investment required to ascertain the preferences of citizens. The reason why more investment is needed for the last task (as γ increases) is simply that the

---

8 To write of parties as if they behaved as individual units, one must, of course, rely on an aggregation procedure. For a more detailed discussion, see Breton, *Economic Theory of Representative Government*, Chapter 7.

more centralized an assignment table is, the more heterogeneous the preferences are likely to be, and the more difficult it is to ascertain them. For the purpose of the analysis of Chapter 7, we will assume that

$$H_{A\gamma}^{G'} = 0. \qquad (5.17)$$

4 THE PREFERENCES OF BUREAUCRATS

In the least-cost model of the assignment and reassignment of functions which we shall develop in Chapter 7, bureaucrats have no role to play; however, in the representative government models of Chapter 8 they will pay a role, and for that reason we introduce them here. We limit ourselves to a brief introduction, reserving the more specific assumptions for the discussion of Chapter 8.

Following some recent work on bureaucracy,[9] we could assume that bureaucrats seek to maximize utility functions defined for one variable, namely power, and go on to approximate the notion of power by a variable such as the size of the budget, or the size of the bureau, or some other measure. We could equivalently assume that the utility functions which bureaucrats seek to maximize are defined for all public policies (S_k), and assume further that the maximum of utility is achieved for a vector of public policies which makes power as large as possible. This second formulation helps focus on the instruments which bureaucrats use, and through which they seek to achieve the implementation of the policies which they desire.[10] In the present context, we find it useful because it makes it easy to define the yield on investment in administration and co-ordination by bureaucrats in a way that is symmetric to the one we have adopted for politicians and citizens in earlier sections of this chapter.

Accordingly, in the discussion of Chapter 8, we will assume that the investment of time and money by governments, in administration and co-ordination activities, is carried out both by politicians and by bureaucrats. For the former the yield on these investments is measured in terms of the value that results from increasing the probability of re-election, while for the latter it is measured in terms of the power which bureaucrats are able to acquire. This will make it possible to derive results which depend on the preferences of bureaucrats.

9 W.A. Niskanen, Jr, *Bureaucracy and Representative Government* (Chicago: Aldine-Atherton 1971); A. Breton and R. Wintrobe, 'The Equilibrium Size of a Budget-Maximizing Bureau: A Note on Niskanen's Theory of Bureaucracy,' *Journal of Political Economy* LXXXIII (February 1975) 195-207

10 The instrument which, in this connection, has most retrained the attention of scholars is the control of information flows. See, for example, G. Tullock, *The Politics of Bureaucracy* (Washington, DC: Public Affairs Press 1965); O.E. Williamson, 'Hierarchical Control and Optimum Firm Size,' *Journal of Political Economy* LXXV 2 (April 1967) 123-38; and A. Breton and R. Wintrobe, 'A Theory of Moral Suasion,' (Toronto: Institute for Policy Analysis 1975) working paper 7514.

6

Constituent assemblies

1 INTRODUCTION

In Chapter 3 we introduced constituent assemblies and defined them as bodies made up of individuals whose tasks are to design the boundaries of jurisdictions and to assign functions to jurisdictional levels. In this chapter, we wish first to distinguish between two different kinds of constituent assemblies and in Section 3 to discuss some of the rules or 'motivations' which, we assume, govern the behaviour of the members of constituent assemblies. In Section 4 we give illustrations of some of the instruments which constituent assemblies use when they decide to alter assignment tables.

Before we proceed with this discussion we must, however, pause to give a name to the members of any constituent assembly. For lack of a better word, we have chosen the French word *constituants*. That was the name taken in 1791 by the members of the French *Etats généraux* meeting under the name of *Assemblée constituante*. The same name was used in 1848-9 and in 1945-6 by members of the *Assemblées constituantes* elected to draft constitutions for the French republics. We use the word in a more abstract and formal sense, but its compactness will serve us well.

2 VARIETIES OF CONSTITUENT ASSEMBLIES

We note at the outset that it is often difficult to identify the real world counterparts of constituent assemblies, since groups meeting to deal with assignment matters are seldom formally called constituent assemblies. One can point to obvious cases such as the meeting in Philadelphia in 1787 and the one in Charlottetown in 1864, but such instances are fairly rare. Sometimes change in the assignment table is undertaken by a federal-provincial committee of first or of other ministers who may or may not be officially and formally meeting for that purpose, but who make changes which are then ratified (or not) by federal and provincial parliaments or sanctioned (or not) by a court. Sometimes the change is worked out in the federal parliament or in congress and is then ratified (or not) by provincial or state legislatures. And sometimes changes in the assignment table are brought about by the decisions of the government of one jurisdiction, as when a provincial government abolishes or creates municipalities or school boards and thus transfers functions to a higher or to a lower level in the jurisdictional hierarchy.

But the assignment table can also be changed by organisms whose resemblance to the notion of a constituent assembly is still more remote than that of the institutions or bodies just described. Indeed, assignment tables can be altered by special-purpose administrative bodies just as they can be by provincial, state, metropolitan, or municipal governments acting unilaterally.

Throughout this study we shall disregard these various idiosyncracies and call any body or group of bodies that reassign functions and redesign the boundaries of jurisdictions a constituent assembly. In building a bridge between the theoretical concept and its real-world counterpart, the empirical investigator will have to deploy the same ingenuity that is required of him or her in other branches of systematic empirical analysis.

We do, however, distinguish between two kinds of constituent assemblies. One we call uni-level and the second multi-level. The first pertains to those bodies in which the *constituants* all come from one jurisdictional level only, while the latter refers to those bodies in which the *constituants* come from two or even three jurisdictional levels in the federation.

Uni-level assemblies are by far the most numerous, since they include most provincial and state governments which usually make unilateral decisions about assignments – that is, decisions which do not formally involve municipal and local governments. In addition, in some countries such as Italy and the United Kingdom, decisions about the assignment of functions are made by the national government. Because the assignment decisions are usually taken by following procedures which are indistinguishable from policy decisions, they receive only limited attention by the public. They are, however, far from trivial.

Multi-level assemblies, bringing together as they do representatives from jurisdictional levels which are most of the time constitutionally independent, make much fewer assignment decisions, but since these involve much bargaining, negotiation, and public posturing receive much more public attention. They are also important, and have to be treated separately from the other type of assembly.

We do not, however, analyse the behaviour of constituent assemblies in which the *constituants* do not formally come from jurisdictional levels, but are drawn from and represent differing regions, occupations, or other estates of society. We recognize that such assemblies have existed, but we note that they have invariably been concerned with initial, and perhaps only formal, assignments – never with reassignment.

3 RULES OF BEHAVIOUR

In the discussion of Chapters 7 and 8, we make only two hypotheses about the behaviour of *constituants*. In the first of these two chapters we assume, in effect, that *constituants*, whether as members of uni- or multi-level assemblies, behave as computers, calculating the cost of the different organizational activities at alternative values of the centralization co-efficient and minimizing these costs. *Constituants* in that chapter have no particular role to play, nor for that matter have constituent assemblies. These assemblies, in their mechanical behaviour, are essentially like the governments postulated by welfare economists or, for that matter, like the median voter so familiar to public choice theorists.

In Chapter 8, *constituants* are assumed to be governed by their own interest. In that chapter, assignment decisions are the outcome of two hypotheses: one which states that elected politicians-as-*constituants* seek their own interest, which is in an important way related to the probability of their re-election; and another which says that bureaucrats as participants in the assignment process also seek their own interest, which in this case is importantly associated with the accumulation of power.[1] It is important for the cases discussed in that chapter to distinguish between uni- and multi-level assemblies.

There is one rule of behaviour or one hypothesis about the behaviour of *constituants* which we do not investigate, but which we mention because of its current popularity. It is the hypothesis that *constituants* act not as computers, but as self-seeking individuals and at the same time make assignment (constitutional) decisions without taking into account the advantages or disadvantages that these decisions have for them. There are a number of assumptions which can be made to eliminate the ill consequences which would otherwise be inherent in the single-minded pursuit of self-interest at the assignment (or constitutional) level. There is the assumption of uncertainty about the *constituants'* future social position used by Buchanan and Tullock;[2] the veil of ignorance about ethically irrelevant information used by Rawls,[3] and finally variants of 'basic' principles such as Kant's categorical imperative.

1 For more detail, the reader is referred to the discussion of Chapter 5.
2 J.M. Buchanan and G. Tullock, *The Calculus of Consent* (Ann Arbor: University of Michigan Press 1962)
3 J. Rawls, *A Theory of Justice* (Cambridge, MA: Harvard University Press 1971)

We do not make use of this general line of argumentation, because it does not appear to us to be of help in understanding the role of the constituent assembly in changing the structure of the public sector. Nor, we believe, would it help us much in defining the rules for the 'best' possible assignment.

4 REASSIGNMENT INSTRUMENTS

What we call the reassignment instruments are the ways and means, the techniques, the procedures, and the rules used by the constituent assembly to change the assignment table; that is, to reassign functions, to redesign the jurisdictional map, or both.

We should note immediately that it is not possible, at any one time, to draw up a list of all possible reassignment instruments, except at a strictly formal level, any more than it is possible to supply a list of all the technologies that could possibly be used to print books. Human beings are creative and often invent new reassignment instruments just as they invent new technologies. It may help the reader, however, if we give a few examples of these instruments.

One way of choosing a new assignment is to change the constitution; that is, to change the legal document which formally contains the design of the boundaries of some jurisdictions and the assignment of some functions to them. The change can be effected in a number of ways, such as by a formal redrafting of the basic document, or by amending it on one or a number of selected issues, or by seeking a reinterpretation of a given clause by appeal to a court. It is important to note that these alternative ways of changing the constitution will usually have different implications in terms of costs and social and constitutional impact.

The reader should also note that changing the constitution, whatever methods are used, is only one instrument for changing the assignment table. The models developed in this book deal with the assignment of functions and only implicitly with constitutional change.

The delegation of a function by constituent assemblies from one jurisdictional level to another is a second reassignment instrument. Such delegation can be upwards or downwards and is not restricted to federal, provincial, and municipal jurisdictional levels, but extends to school boards, to metropolitan, and to regional levels. There has historically been enough delegation of powers from one jurisdictional level to another that one need not underline the importance of this instrument. In terms of the distinction between uni- and multi-level assemblies, delegation of powers is an instrument that will usually be used by the latter for reasons that will become apparent in the next paragraph.

Many times, however, what appears as a delegation of authority is essentially the take-over of a function by a government acting as a uni-level constituent assembly. The main difference between delegation and take-over of functions arises from the fact that uni-level assemblies have in themselves the constitutional authority to reassign functions which governments in countries with multi-level assemblies do not. For example, in Canada the federal government does not have the constitutional authority to reassign functions unilaterally between itself and the provinces, while the provinces have this power vis-à-vis the municipalities.

In connection with our foregoing listing we can also note the modification of political boundaries and the creation of function-specific political jurisdictions such as school boards or metropolitan governments. If we recall the definition of the assignment table given in Chapter 3, it becomes clear that functions will always be reassigned when the jurisdictional map is redesigned, even if the opposite is not true. Indeed, if a given territory is completely mapped out from a political point of view, a change in political boundaries which can only be achieved by enlarging a jurisdiction at the expense of another is thus equivalent to reassigning functions. In principle, political boundaries are defined for each specific function, so that it is possible to extend the boundaries of one jurisdiction for one function while curtailing them for another.[4]

It is, of course, true that the boundaries of provincial and state jurisdictions are not often altered, but those of municipal and metropolitan jurisdictions as well as those of school boards do get changed, so that the redesign of jurisdictional maps is an instrument used to reassign functions.

In concluding this section, we wish to re-emphasize the supremacy of the constituent assembly in matters of assignment. It has full authority to adopt and to alter reassignment instruments, including its own procedures and rules. In the analysis that follows we assume these rules to be given, but there is no doubt that in practice rules and procedures are changed. But that is another subject.

5 CONCLUSION

There is one aspect of constituent assemblies which we have not yet mentioned. These are the conditions under which assemblies will initially be convened. They

4 An extreme version of this possibility is illustrated in Figure 3.1 of Chapter 3. Columns 5, 6, 7, and 8 can be interpreted as showing the effects on γ of four alternative positions of the provincial boundaries among the jurisdictions for different functions. In column 5, all functions are performed (equally) by 48 states. In column 6, the 48 states are combined into six for 50 per cent of the functions and into 24 for the remaining half. Columns 7 and 8 show other percentages. These last two alternatives can be interpreted as having six out of 24 states completely take over the provision of certain functions, but not others.

appear to be conditions that are difficult to identify or classify precisely. Indeed, they are the dynamic conditions which lead to the formation of federations and states. The models that follow presuppose the existence of political states and of some initial structure of governments. This does not imply that, interpreted in a different light, our models could not be used to explain which new states have chosen, or had chosen for them, a federal form in the first place.

7

Least-cost models of federalism

1 INTRODUCTION

In the previous two chapters we have introduced the actors and institutions – citizens, governments, and constituent assemblies[1] – whose actions always determine the assignment of functions or powers between jurisdictional levels. In this chapter, holding to the objective functions imputed to citizens and governments, we work through the implications of the hypothesis that constituent assemblies act in such a way as to minimize the sum total of resources invested in organizational activities, that is in mobility, signalling, administration, and co-ordination by citizens and governments. Except when otherwise indicated, we assume that changes in the assignment table can be effected by constituent assemblies at no cost, or to put it differently, we assume that the costs of using the reassignment instruments are zero. We also assume that citizens and governments reveal their investment decisions to the constituent assembly without requiring this body to use up resources searching for these decisions.

In this cost minimization model, neither the constituent assembly, nor the citizens, nor the politicians have preferences about the assignment of powers between jurisdictional levels. The constituent assembly more or less as a computational device grinds out the implication of particular assumptions and reassigns functions as the data change. One of the great virtues of this construct over alternatives is that the specific content of different assumptions about the behaviour of citizens and governments is clearly brought out. In addition, it provides the groundwork on which different models of federalism can be erected.

To proceed, we describe, in the next section, the nature of the equilibrium as-

---

1 Both governments and constituent assemblies, it will be recalled, are composed of politicians and bureaucrats.

signment that results when the constituent assembly is assumed to minimize organizational costs. Then in Section 3 we analyse a number of comparative statical displacements from equilibrium and make some predictions on how the system will adjust. In Section 4, we derive the implications of the least-cost model for questions such as fiscal responsibility and minimum standards which have been traditional issues in the literature of federalism. Finally, in Section 5, we examine how, even under the simplifications of cost minimization, it is possible to obtain a misassignment of functions.

2 THE NATURE OF THE LEAST-COST EQUILIBRIUM

To proceed with the analysis, we break the assignment problem down into three parts and examine each in turn. In the first subsection, we describe the reaction or *tâtonnement* process that underlies the least-cost model; in the second subsection we state the conditions that have to be met if the equilibrium is to be a stable one; and in the last subsection we examine certain properties of the equilibrium with special reference to its capacity to endure through time and hence with reference to the durability of an assignment that could have been initially imposed by history, geography, or other similar 'causes.'

The tâtonnement process
The reader will recall that the variable over which the constituent assembly has control is the centralization co-efficient (γ), or equivalently, the assignment of functions or powers, or the structure of the public sector. We begin by assuming that the constituent assembly plays a role similar to that of Walras's *crieur*. In that capacity, it meets, as it were, with all the governments and asks them a question like the following: if citizens decide to invest a certain quantum of resources in political mobility, what amount would you yourselves invest in co-ordination activities, assuming the centralization co-efficient (γ) and the market rate of interest (i) to be given?[2] A similar question would be asked for every alternative amount of investment in political mobility by citizens. The various answers could then be plotted and the locus of points called a reaction function. The same kind of exercise would be performed for investment in signalling. Then the constituent assembly would meet the citizens and ask them a similar question, though this time the answer sought would be for their investment in mobility (and signalling) for alternative government investments in administration and co-ordination.

2 The reader should recall that the cost of organizational activities is given, and as a consequence the above question can be formulated in terms of the amounts of investments involved.

Because of the assumptions we feel justified in making, the number of questions that have to be asked and answered or the number of reaction functions (R) that have to be specified can be reduced to four: two for governments and two for citizens. They are the following:

$$H_E^G = R_E^G(H_Z^C, \bar{\rho}_{H_E}, \bar{\gamma}_0) \tag{7.1}$$

$$H_A^G = R_A^G(H_Z^C, \bar{\rho}_{H_A}, \bar{\gamma}_0) \tag{7.2}$$

$$H_\mu^C = R_\mu^C(H_B^G, \bar{\rho}_{H_\mu}, \bar{\gamma}_0) \tag{7.3}$$

$$H_\sigma^C = R_\sigma^C(H_B^G, \bar{\rho}_{H_\sigma}, \bar{\gamma}_0) \tag{7.4}$$

where

$$H_Z^C = H_\mu^C + H_\sigma^C \tag{7.5}$$

and

$$H_B^G = H_A^G + H_E^G \tag{7.6}$$

and where C and G stand for the sum over all citizens and governments respectively; and the bars over the ρ's and γ's indicate that they are held constant. Equation (7.1) can be read as follows: R_E^G describes how investment in E by governments (H_E^G) varies when investment in Z by citizens (H_Z^C) is altered, holding constant the internal rate of return on E as well as the degree of centralization. A similar interpretation of (7.2), (7.3), and (7.4) holds *mutatis mutandis*.

The reduction in the number of reaction functions – answers to the type of questions formulated above – from a possible eight to four follows from (7.5) and (7.6). Are we allowed these sums? Equation (7.6) seems easy to justify. Indeed, it seems reasonable to assume that citizens do not have views or care about how a government proceeds to reduce the degree of frustration to which they are subjected, whether that be through co-ordination of the activities that generate interactions of various types, or whether it be by searching for better ways of doing what they are already doing, or by searching for information on tastes, or something else. In other words, if frustration is reduced that will satisfy citizens. Sum (7.5) is more difficult to rationalize in the terms we have just used to justify (7.6). We make it on the grounds that the reaction co-efficients of governments – the first derivative of $R_{E\mu}^G, R_{E\sigma}^G$, etc. – with respect to H_μ and H_σ are likely to have the same sign. Should that not be the case the analysis that follows would be more involved, but its nature would not be altered.

To proceed, we need to make assumptions on how governments will alter their investments in co-ordination or administration or both when citizens alter their own investments in mobility, signalling, or both, and on how citizens will change their own investments in organizational activities when governments alter theirs. To put it differently, we need to formulate assumptions about whether investments in co-ordination and administration are substitutes for, complements to, or independent of investments in mobility and signalling both from the citizens' and the governments' viewpoint.

To proceed, we make the following assumptions, though the reader can easily verify for him- or herself that many other assumptions are possible and consistent with the analysis below. We suppose that

$$R_{EZ}^{G'} > 0, \tag{7.7}$$

$$R_{AZ}^{G'} = 0, \tag{7.8}$$

$$R_{\mu B}^{C'} < 0, \tag{7.9}$$

and

$$R_{OB}^{C'} < 0 \tag{7.10}$$

where $R_{EZ}^{G'} \equiv \partial R_E^G / \partial H_Z^C$, etc. In other words, we assume in (7.7) that when citizens increase their investments in mobility, signalling, or both, governments will decide to increase their investment in co-ordination. We could then say that these two kinds of investments – signalling and mobility by citizens and co-ordination by governments – are complements.

The assumed sign of $R_{AZ}^{G'}$ can be rationalized as follows. If citizens participate more in the political process they reveal more and more clearly what their preferences are and as a consequence less search is required by governments, but other policies or different amounts of the existing policies have to be implemented and this requires more of the other kinds of administrative activities. Our assumption that $R_{AZ}^{G'} = 0$ is equivalent to the assumption that these effects exactly cancel out. If they do not, $R_{AZ}^{G'}$ would be either positive or negative without in any way altering the logic of the argument.

We set $R_{\mu B}^{C'} < 0$ and $R_{OB}^{C'} < 0$, by reasoning that from the citizens' point of view co-ordination and administration are substitutes for mobility and signalling, that is, that less of the latter are needed to achieve the same reduction in coercion when more of the former are provided by governments. As already indicated these are specific assumptions made for illustrative purposes. Others could be made and in the next sections we ourselves sometimes make different assumptions.

Using assumptions (7.7 to 7.10), we draw Figure 7.1 and note that for a given market rate of interest and centralization co-efficient, the equilibrium is at D[3]

3 At D, in other words, the investment behaviour of citizens is consistent with that of governments and vice versa. If the reaction of citizens lagged that of governments, or

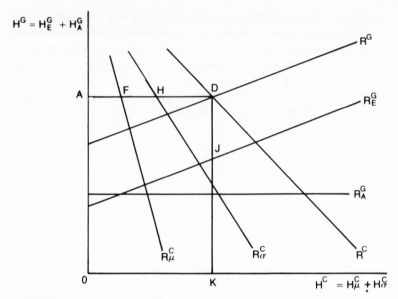

Figure 7.1

given by the intersection of R^G (the vertical sum of R_A^G and R_E^G) and R^C (the horizontal sum of R_μ^C and R_σ^C). At that point the total amount of resources invested in organization by governments is KD $(=OA)$ divided in co-ordination (KJ) and administration (JD), and the total amount invested by citizens is AD $(=OK)$ broken down in AF of mobility and AH of signalling. The total amount of resources used up in operating the public sector (in addition, of course, to the resources used in producing policies) is $OA + OK$ $(=H^* = H^{C*} + H^{G*})$.

Before examining how this last sum varies when γ is altered the reader should recall that at D the following equality holds (at least as long as we assume a perfect capital market):

$$\sigma_{H_\mu} = \sigma_{H_\sigma} = \sigma_{H_E} = \sigma_{H_A} = i \qquad (7.11)$$

or, to put it in words, the internal rate of return on every investment is equal and equal to the market rate of interest. Why? Because at every point along the reaction curves, each agent – citizens or governments – invests up to the point where

if the reaction of governments lagged that of citizens, point D would be stable only if the slope of R^C taken with respect to the H^G-axis was smaller than that of R^G, a standard cobweb phenomenon.

the internal rate of return on the investment considered is equal to i. They must therefore all be equal at D.

Let us now examine what happens when the centralization co-efficient γ is varied by the constituent assembly. To do this we use assumptions (5.10), (5.11), (5.16), and (5.17) from above. To repeat, these are

$$H_{\mu\gamma}^{C'} < 0 \tag{5.10}$$

$$H_{\sigma\gamma}^{C'} > 0 \tag{5.11}$$

$$H_{E\gamma}^{G'} < 0 \tag{5.16}$$

and

$$H_A^{G'} = 0 \tag{5.17}$$

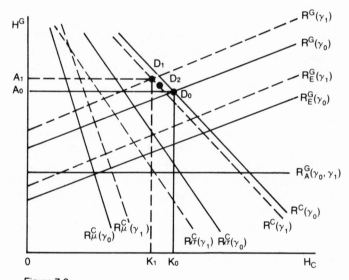

Figure 7.2

We proceed by redrawing Figure 7.1 as Figure 7.2, and imagine that γ is lowered from γ_0 to γ_1, that is, that the degree of centralization of the public sector is reduced. The total amount of resources allocated to the organization of the public sector changes from $OA_0 + OK_0$ to $OA_1 + OK_1$. Inspection of Figure 7.2 reveals that in this particular case, $K_0 - K_1 > A_1 - A_0$ that is, less resources are used for organizational purposes with γ_1 than with γ_0, so that the constituent assembly – given that it seeks to minimize organization costs – will choose γ_1 instead of γ_0. This should become immediately obvious to the reader if he recalls that at γ_1, the market rate of interest which ruled with γ_0 still obtains and that equality (7.11) therefore also still holds.

The constituent assembly will now experiment with further values of γ, and, as it has just done, calculate the total cost of resources invested in organization by all parties and select the γ – call it γ^* – which makes H a minimum – call it H^*. This is the equilibrium γ corresponding to an equilibrium assignment table Ω^* or alternatively, the γ that corresponds to an equilibrium structure of the public sector in the least-cost model.[4]

The reader should have no difficulty in convincing himself that the particular assumptions embedded in (5.10), (5.11), (5.16), and / or (5.17) can be altered. Indeed, a change in one or all of these assumptions would be represented in Figure 7.2 by different shifts of the reaction functions as γ was varied. Suppose, to illustrate, that when γ fell from γ_0 to γ_1, investment in administration by governments did not remain unchanged, but decreased – that is, suppose $H_{A\gamma}^{G'} < 0$ – then the R^G curve could still move outwards, but by a smaller amount (say) and the equilibrium would be at a point such as D_2. We must, however, if stability is to be ensured, impose restrictions on the changes in signs that are permissible. These restrictions are spelled out in the next subsection.

The stability conditions

Before we do this for the general case, however, the reader should note that for the special case of Figure 7.2 the process described will only produce γ's that are equal to zero or to one, unless we impose stability conditions on the equilibrating process. To put it differently, given only the assumptions (5.10), (5.11), (5.16), and (5.17), a decrease in γ that leads to a reduction in resources allocated to organizational activities will produce reductions for all lower γ's until $\gamma = 0$ is reached. Similarly, increases in γ that produced reductions in resource use will stop only when that co-efficient is equal to one. The system would be unstable. To guarantee stability we require that if

$$\left| \frac{\partial^2 H_\mu^C}{\partial \gamma^2} \right| - \left| \frac{\partial^2 H_\sigma^C}{\partial \gamma^2} \right| > 0 \tag{7.12}$$

then

$$\left| \frac{\partial^2 H_A^G}{\partial \gamma^2} \right| - \left| \frac{\partial^2 H_E^G}{\partial \gamma^2} \right| < 0 \tag{7.13}$$

---

4 We remind the reader that in general it is not possible to go from a given γ to a unique Ω, and that as a consequence the above statements hold only for special cases.

or, conversely, if

$$\left|\frac{\partial^2 H_\mu^C}{\partial\gamma^2}\right| - \left|\frac{\partial^2 H_\sigma^C}{\partial\gamma^2}\right| < 0 \tag{7.14}$$

stability will obtain only if

$$\left|\frac{\partial^2 H_A^G}{\partial\gamma^2}\right| - \left|\frac{\partial^2 H_E^G}{\partial\gamma^2}\right| > 0. \tag{7.15}$$

In words, given the assumptions of equations (5.10), (5.11), (5.16), and (5.17), these conditions state that if γ decreases and if investment in mobility on the part of citizens increases at a faster (slower) rate than the rate at which investment in signalling is falling, then investment in co-ordination by governments must increase at a faster (slower) rate than the rate at which investment in administration is reduced.

The above conditions could obviously also be stated in the following alternative form: if (7.13) [or (7.15)] obtains, the equilibrium will be stable only if (7.12) [or (7.14)] holds. The conditions are perfectly symmetric.

If stability is guaranteed by equations (7.12) and (7.13), the behaviour of $H(=H^G + H^C)$ as γ varies can be represented in a diagram such as Figure 7.3,

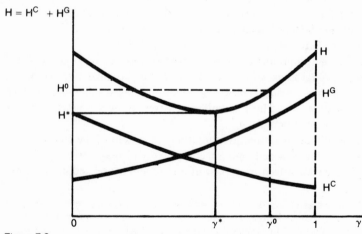

Figure 7.3

which incorporates these stability conditions. (If (7.14) and (7.15) obtain, another diagram, with the curves reversed but completely symmetric to Figure 7.3, is needed.)

Our specific assumptions (5.10), (5.11), (5.16), and (5.17) have hidden a very important phenomenon. Indeed, they have hidden the fact that our stability conditions hold and have meaning if and only if, when γ increases (say), a reduction in investment in organizational activities by citizens is matched by an increase in investment in administration and co-ordination by governments and *vice versa* for an increase in signalling and mobility. To put it differently, in a slightly inexact but instructive way, in our least-cost model organizational investments by governments are substitutes for organizational investments by citizens and *vice versa*. To stay with that language, if these two kinds of activities were complements, the structure would be unstable in the sense that it would go either towards zero (Balkanization) or towards one (unitary structure).[5]

What kind of assumptions we wish to make about investment in signalling, mobility, administration, and co-ordination as γ changes will depend on the facts. These may be consistent with a stable structure of the public sector, but then they may not and in those cases we should observe a structure resembling one or the other of the two possible extremes.

The equilibrium assignment

Once γ* has been determined, net investment in mobility and signalling by citizens and in co-ordination and administration by governments will be zero, though gross investment will still be positive. In equilibrium, to put it differently, citizens will have chosen a desired location consistent with the flow of resources over which they have command, and / or they will have signalled their preferences to their governments and will not invest more in these activities. Similarly, governments will have reached agreements, set up machinery, and signed contracts to deal with interjurisdictional interactions and interdependencies.

Both citizens and governments, however, will allocate resources to the maintenance of their capital stock, to what in effect, in this particular case, we should call the enforcement of the agreements, contracts, promises, and understandings that have been achieved and which underlie the pattern of public policy provision which has been decided upon.

The reader should be aware that in equilibrium, as a result of the co-ordination services that are being provided and as a consequence of these services, a federal structure will be characterized by a flow of intergovernmental and interjurisdic-

---

5 We do not pursue here the relationship between assignment instability and complementarity of investments by citizens and governments. But we note that it is an interesting and intriguing relationship. For example, it says that a federal structure in which assignments are governed by minimum-cost considerations would be unstable if signalling by citizens induced search by governments, which in turn provoked more signalling by citizens. Such a phenomenon could be brought about if search activity elicited partial, biased, or distorted information about the source of the coercion motivating signalling.

tional payments, which are in effect payments for intergovernmental trade in public policies. To put it differently, the formulation of contracts and of other agreements to deal with interjurisdictional interactions and interdependencies necessarily implies a flow of funds between the governments of a federation.

Furthermore, we can note that many of these payments may, to reduce the co-ordination costs, take an institutional form that makes them look very much like grants. To the extent that these contractual payments can be called grants, they would not be payments for non-market interactions, and consequently would not achieve the goals of co-ordination. To the extent, therefore, that the intergovernmental grants that we observe in federal structures are contractual payments it is wrong to argue that they should be unconditional. To make them so would only worsen the allocation of resources.[6]

We must now drop the assumption that the constituent assembly can reassign functions costlessly. For that purpose, assume that at a certain time the assignment table that is observed in a given society is Ω^0, corresponding to γ^0 in Figure 7.3. That assignment represents a higher degree of centralization than the equilibrium assignment and as a consequence investment at a rate of $H^0 (>H^*)$ is being undertaken.

That initial assignment Ω^0 could have been brought about by a war, or by a historical accident, such as its imposition by a foreign imperial power; or it could have been the result of opposition between such groups as the *Girondins* and the *Jacobins*[7] during a confrontation in which one group was able to totally dominate the other.

Whatever the reason for the existence of $\Omega^0(\neq\Omega^*)$, the question that we must answer is whether the constituent assembly would move to Ω^*. The answer depends on the cost of using the reassignment instruments, which until now we have assumed to be zero. If the costs are positive, however, the constituent assembly will move to Ω^* only if they are less than the savings that this move made possible $(H^0 - H^*)$.

3 SOME COMPARATIVE STATICAL RESULTS

To derive comparative statical results that could be applied to particular federal structures would require more empirical knowledge than we now possess. We would, to be exact, need information about how the position and slopes of the H^C and H^G curves in Figure 7.3 change when there is an exogenous change in

---

6 See Chapter 12 for a more complete discussion of this question.
7 The reader will recall that during the French Revolution the former favoured decentralization, while the latter supported centralization.

data. For example, one would like to know, among other things, the extent of past capital accumulation in and therefore that capital intensity of each organizational activity. One would also like to know the size of the response of investment in each of the organizational activities to changes in the market rate of interest.

With such information it would be possible to predict how the slope of the H^C and H^G curves change as γ changes. For example, it would be possible to be certain that the ratio of investment in co-ordination to investment in administration falls as γ increases, and also about the behaviour of the slope of the H^G curve for all values of γ when the system is submitted to an external disturbance.

In the absence of firm empirical knowledge about these various elasticities, ratios, etc., the only alternative is to proceed by making assumptions and guesses about them to illustrate the kind of analysis that is possible.

In the subsections that follow, we illustrate the workings of the model by analysing how, from an initial equilibrium, the assignment table is changed (1) when the market rate of interest changes; (2) when a tax is imposed on signalling; (3) when the life expectancy of populations differs; and (4) when new public policies are introduced. These do not exhaust the list of possible comparative statical exercises that one can engage in, but it should be sufficient to indicate the flavour as well as the power of the least-cost model developed in this chapter.

In applying the comparative statical predictions formulated below, the reader may sometimes wish to proceed by comparing situations at two different points in time – that is, in the terms in which the analysis below is generally conducted – but he may also wish to compare situations in two different societies at the same point in time. Though the two exercises are not strictly equivalent, they are similar enough to be two legitimate applications of the model.

Variations in the market rate of interest
The market rate of interest that is relevant for the present analysis is the permanent long-term real rate of interest, by which we mean the rate of interest – corrected for expected price changes – about which the measured long-term market rates oscillate.

Consider a country in which the permanent long-term interest rate has moved from one position to another higher one. Assuming, as is usual, that the response of investment to a higher interest rate is negative, the assumed change will lead to a reduction in investment in all organizational activities. The exact reduction in these activities will depend on the size of the elasticities of the component investment schedules at the relevant interest rate.

To examine the effect of such a reduction in investment by citizens (H^C) and by governments (H^G) on the equilibrium value of the centralization co-efficient,

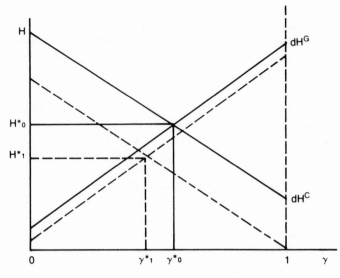

Figure 7.4

we assume that the total investment functions portrayed in Figure 7.3 of Section 2 - in which investment is dependent on γ - are quadratic equations so that their marginals are linear. We represent these marginal curves in Figure 7.4. Shifts in these marginal curves, it should be noted, are caused by changes in the slopes of the total curves. The degree of centralization that minimizes total resource cost is then equal to γ_0^*, the co-efficient that equalizes the marginal rate of investment by citizens to that by governments, and which is the same as the γ^* of Figure 7.3.

To analyse the effects on γ of an increase in i, we must know how the slopes of the (total) H^C and H^G curves are affected. In the absence of empirical data, we conjecture that the interest elasticity of investment in mobility and signalling is larger at lower values of γ than at higher values. One possible justification of this conjecture is that investment in mobility is more interest elastic than investment in signalling, and that the ratio of the former to the latter falls as γ increases. Under these conditions an increase in i will cause the H^C curve in Figure 7.3 to become flatter and the dH^C curve - the marginal curve - in Figure 7.4 to shift downwards.

If, by similar reasoning about the components of governmental organizational activities, the H^G curve becomes flatter, then the dH^G curve will also shift downwards. Whether the resulting value of γ will be to the right or to the left of γ_0^* will depend on the relative magnitudes of these two shifts. Figure 7.4 portrays a situation where the only important effect of an increase in i is that conjectured in the preceeding paragraph. As can be seen, the large shift in the dH^C curve relative to that of the dH^G curve causes γ to fall from γ_0^* to γ_1^*.

Changes in the cost of organizational activities
The analysis of this subsection could be conducted by focusing on any one of the factors that enter into the production of organizational activities. We could, for example, assume an improvement in the technology, or a change in the price of labour, or of capital, or in a number of other dimensions influencing the cost side of organization. The analysis that follows would proceed along the same lines whatever variable that affected costs had been chosen for discussion.

For the purpose of this subsection, we simply assume that the cost of engaging in one particular activity – signalling – has been changed by the introduction of a tax on the performance of that activity. To proceed, we picture a curve representing varying numbers of signals a citizen or a group of citizens 'emits' as the price of signals (q) varies. This is a derived demand curve for signals (s), since it is derived from a desire to reduce or eliminate the coercion that has been imposed on those citizens by public policies.[8] The curve is pictured in Figure 7.5. At the

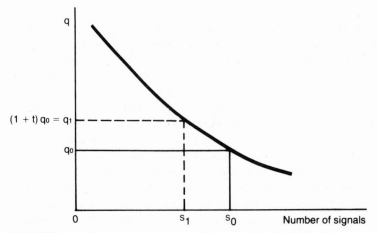

Figure 7.5

---

8 The factors that determine the elasticity of any derived demand curve at any point are the elasticity of the demand curve for public policies, the elasticity of substitution between the various organizational activities, and the fraction of the total costs of organizational activities accounted for by a given activity such as signalling. See A. Marshall, *Principles of Economics*, 8th ed. (New York: Macmillan 1920) Book V, Chapter 6, 385-6; also J.R. Hicks, *The Theory of Wages* (London: Macmillan 1963) 373-8.

initial price for signals of q_0, citizens buy s_0 signals and invest a sum equal to $0q_0a_0s_0$ in signalling. After the introduction of the tax, the price increases to q_1, the quantity demanded falls to s_1, and the sum invested goes to $0q_1a_1s_1$. Whether the volume of investment increases, remains constant, or falls as a result of the tax depends on the price elasticity of the derived demand curve at q_0.

To simplify the exposition, we assume that the tax leads to a fall in the sum invested in signalling. That information, however, is not sufficient to derive comparative statical results with respect to γ. Information is also required about changes in the slopes of both the H^C and H^G curves when investment in signalling changes. If we still assume, as in the previous subsection, that the ratio of investment in mobility to investment in signalling falls as γ increases, then the H^C curve will flatten out as the tax on signalling increases.

In the case of the H^G curve, a tax on signalling will lead to a bodily shift of the curve downwards, as can be verified with Figure 7.2. The slope of that curve will, however, remain unchanged. Consequently the marginal of the H^G curve will not shift. The above statement extends beyond the case of a tax on signalling. Any exogenous change that alters investment by citizens in mobility, or signalling, or both will alter the level but not the slope of the H^G curve, and *vice versa*. Thus the marginal curves are independent of each other.

In the particular case of tax on signalling, the only change in the marginal curves is a downward movement in the dH^C curve of Figure 7.4, and consequently the equilibrium value of γ falls.

There is no need to examine how γ changes when (because of an elasticity of derived demand at q_0 which is less than one) investment in signalling increases as a result of a tax on signals: the analysis holds *mutatis mutandis*.

Differences in life expectancy

Though the principles that apply in comparing two societies in which the life expectancy at birth differs are essentially the same as the ones outlined in the last subsection, it will illustrate the nature of the least-cost model anew to spell out the predictions it contains.

Assume therefore two societies in which the average life expectancy at birth is substantially different or assume a significant change in the average life expectancy in a given society. Assume further, in accordance with the findings of theoretical and empirical research on capital formation in human beings,[9] combined with the results of research on life-cycle and consumption patterns,[10] that indivi-

---

9 See, for example, Y. Ben-Porath, 'The Production of Human Capital and the Life-Cycle of Earnings,' *Journal of Political Economy* (August 1967) or J. Mincer, National Bureau of Economic Research, *Schooling, Experience, and Earnings* (New York: Columbia University Press 1974).

10 F. Modigliani and R. Brumberg, 'Utility Analysis and the Consumption Function: An

duals with a longer life expectancy generally save and invest more and consequently invest more in themselves in the form of education and health than individuals with a shorter life expectancy. It seems reasonable to suppose that they also invest more in political signalling and in political mobility.[11]

Because the effect of the increase in H^C on the equilibrium value of γ depends on the change in the slope of the H^C curve, we must investigate whether the increase in investment in mobility is greater or smaller than that in signalling. To do this, we make two assumptions: first, we suppose, as we did above, that the ratio of investment in mobility to that in signalling falls as γ increases, and second, we assume that an increase in life expectancy increases the profitability of signalling more than that of mobility, and consequently that the mobility-signalling mix moves in favour of signalling.

This second assumption seems plausible because an increase in life expectancy enables citizens, at the margin of choosing between mobility and signalling, to wait for the delayed benefits of signalling which they previously did not expect to receive during their lifetime. With a shorter life expectancy, the more immediate benefits of mobility were more attractive.

The combined effect of these two assumptions is that an increase in life expectancy will make the H^C curve steeper as γ increases.

Turning now to the H^G curve, it seems difficult to imagine that an increase in life expectancy will have a predictable effect on the administration–co-ordination mix. If, however, we conjecture that the benefits accruing from administration activities are more immediate in time than those from co-ordination, an increase in life expectancy will induce more investment in co-ordination. If the ratio of investment in this activity to investment in administration falls as γ rises, the H^G curve will become flatter.

The steeper H^C curve and flatter H^G curve imply that the equilibrium value of γ increases with an increase in life expectancy.

This is not a trivial proposition. It can be used, albeit with caution, to explain what Peacock and Wiseman call the 'concentration process,' that is, 'the change in the relative importance of central and local levels of government.'[12] We assume

Interpretation of Cross-Section Data,' in K.K. Kurihara, *Post-Keynesian Economics* (New Brunswick, NJ: Rutgers University Press 1954) or A. Ando and F. Modigliani, 'The Life-Cycle Hypothesis of Saving: Aggregate Implications and Tests,' *American Economic Review* (March 1963) 53-84

11 We assume that governments in societies where life expectancy is longer do not invest less or more in administration and co-ordination than those where life expectancy is shorter.

12 A.T. Peacock and J. Wiseman, *The Growth of Public Expenditure in the United Kingdom* (London: Allen and Unwin 1967) 118

for the United States – a country for which data are readily available – that the permanent long-term rate of interest has been constant over the last 75 to 100 years – an assumption that does not square completely with the facts, but one which is not too far off either[13] – and also that life expectancy at birth in that country has been rising, an assumption that is consistent with the facts.[14] On these assumptions, the least-cost model predicts a tendency towards a more concentrated public sector, a tendency which is always difficult to document,[15] but which seems to be present in this case.[16]

New policies
Under this heading we deal with the situation that arises when, as a result of changes in the technology of producing private or public goods, or as a result of changes in the characteristics of commodities, or finally as a result of changes in preferences, new public policies have to be introduced or old ones changed. A good illustration of what we have in mind is the change occurring in the television industry from off-the-air to cable TV. We will suggest that when TV signals are picked off-the-air, the power to regulate TV will be assigned to the central government by a resource minimizing constituent assembly, whereas when TV signals are carried by cables the same power will be assigned to provincial governments.

Our reason for this suggestion is that the change in technology reduces co-ordination costs. Indeed, cable TV, because it generates no spill-overs, does not require any co-ordination by governments, whereas off-the-air TV generates the conflicts of any common-property resource. It follows from the least-cost model that a reduction in investment in co-ordination, investment in other organizational activities remaining unchanged, would make the H^G curve steeper. The reason for this is that the ratio of investment in co-ordination to investment in administration under the older technology declined as γ increased. With the new technology this rate of decline will be much smaller.

13 See, for example, M. Friedman and A. Schwartz, National Bureau of Economic Research, *A Monetary History of the United States, 1867–1960* (Princeton: Princeton University Press 1963) 640.
14 *Social Indicators, 1973* (Washington, DC: Government Printing Office, Statistical Policy Division, Office of Management and Budget 1973) 2
15 Note that in some countries like Canada in recent years the concentration process appears to fit the facts of the relative change in the importance of provincial compared to municipal governments, but not of the federal compared to the provincial level. When two opposite trends operate in this way, it is still possible for one index – the γ coefficient – to rise, even though the interpretation of the rise may be difficult. See, for example, R.M. Bird, *The Growth of Government Spending in Canada* (Toronto: Canadian Tax Foundation 1970), esp. Chapter 9.
16 See the numbers we present in Chapter 3, Section 4. See also F.L. Pryor, *Public Expenditures in Communist and Capitalist Nations* (London: Allen and Unwin 1968) 72.

Unless there are special reasons to believe that the introduction of the new technology will change the slope of the H^C curve, the only outcome of that change will be a downward shift of the entire H^C curve, with no change in its marginal.

If the slope of the H^C curve remains unchanged, and that of the H^G curve increases for all values of γ, it follows that the effect of the replacement of off-the-air broadcasting by cable TV will be to reduce the equilibrium value of γ.

To put it differently and more generally, with each type of commodities and with each technology and preference structure is associated a bundle of policies to which is associated in turn a vector of investment-in-organization levels which, given the market rate of interest and the real alternative cost of resources, helps determine the size of the centralization co-efficient. A change in the nature of a commodity, in the structure of preferences, and / or in technology which requires a change in policy bundles will also require an alternative vector of investment-in-organizational-activities level – some elements of which may rise and others fall – which will induce a cost-minimizing constituent assembly to alter γ to insure that the internal rate of return on each investment remains equal to the unchanged market rate of interest.

4 SOME APPLICATIONS OF THE LEAST-COST MODEL

In Part Three of this book we deal with some of the classically important problems of federalism – redistribution, stabilization, and intergovernmental grants. In this section, we simply look at the light which the least-cost model can shed on a few problems which have often attracted the attention of students of federalism. They are: fiscal responsibility, national minimum standards, and the geographical distribution of the population. We examine each in turn.

Fiscal responsibility
One issue that has attracted the attention of public finance economists, as well as of accountants and lawyers interested in federalism, is the question of fiscal responsibility. That issue, or to put it differently, fiscal irresponsibility, can take two different forms. It can originate from the presence of 'perverse' inducements or incentives in the system of intergovernmental grants. It can also originate from the fact that the governments who spend the money are not always those which collect it. Though these two sources of irresponsibility have been discussed separately in the literature, they are obviously similar to each other.

In this connection, it is interesting to recall the empirical literature on the effects of government grants on local expenditure patterns.[17] That literature has

17 For example, E.M. Gramlich, 'Alternative Federal Policies for Stimulating State and

devoted substantial attention to the measurement of the displacement and distortion effects of higher-level government grants on lower-level government expenditure patterns and in particular on the extent to which junior governments are induced to spend some of their own funds on policies they would not have otherwise financed and away from their own priorities. Although that is not the usual meaning given to the notion of fiscal irresponsibility, it is appropriate in the least-cost model to say that it is the obverse image of the phenomenon described in the preceding paragraph and as a consequence it is possible to interpret that literature as providing us with a measure of one aspect of fiscal irresponsibility.

In all cases, fiscal irresponsibility would be completely removed if organizational costs were zero; it is a necessary consequence of positive organizational costs. For example, the cost of collecting taxes leading to centralization of revenue functions with payments of the proceeds to other levels, already removes the identity of tax collector and revenue spender, and is thus a source of fiscal irresponsibility. Similarly, the cost of co-ordination between governments leading to lack of agreement also leads to fiscal irresponsibility.

Minimum standards and concurrent authority
It is fair to say that, on the whole, public finance economists and other students of federalism have not paid much attention to the question of concurrent authority – the phenomenon that appears when a function is assigned to two or more jurisdictional levels – and in particular have not asked why it exists. The same is true of national (or provincial, etc.) minimum standards, for the provision of certain services, except that in this case, economists in particular have argued that they exist for distributional reasons, are essentially arbitrary, and imply a departure from maximum efficiency. Minimum standards, the argument goes, would not be observed if the distribution of income was optimal according to some criterion, or if income could be redistributed in lump-sum fashion.

Both concurrent authority and minimum standards can be understood by reference to our model of a constituent assembly assigning functions in such a way as to minimize the use of resources for organizational purposes. These devices will be adopted whenever the costs of co-ordination activities are low enough to permit the formulation and development of contractual payment schemes that go in the direction of internalizing some of the existing interjurisdictional spillovers and externalities and of exploiting some of the interjurisdictional economies of scale.

Local Expenditures: A Comparison of Their Effects,' *National Tax Journal* XXI 2 (June 1968) 119-29

Let us focus on minimum standards first and then move on to concurrent authority. To understand the origin and purpose of minimum standards it is sufficient to recognize that these standards are relatively easy to devise and to agree on. They are usually defined in terms of a relatively simple index such as the amount of a particular service per person. Once the standard is defined and accepted, and some minimum limit set and agreed upon, the task of working out the size and characteristics of the contractual payments between governments is greatly simplified, and indeed, becomes almost mechanical.

What the cost-minimizing model suggests therefore is that national or other minimum standards of provision for certain public services serve to reduce the amount of resources used up in co-ordination activities and therefore make it possible for governments to exploit a larger proportion of potential economies of scale and to internalize a larger fraction of interdependencies in private and public goods supply.

Our understanding of minimum standards, and also of contractual payments, can be improved by asking why these standards do not exist for all public services, but are limited to a subset of them. Minimum standards will exist when it is possible to devise an easily ascertainable index which allows co-ordination of activities which would otherwise be ruled out because of the high cost of co-ordination. To put it differently, if it is easy to devise and agree on an index that defines standards, the costs of co-ordination will be lowered sufficiently to allow the constituent assembly to decentralize the strucutre of the public sector more than the minimization of total organizational resource cost would otherwise permit. If the lowering of co-ordination costs cannot be achieved in this way the entire function will be assigned to a higher jurisdictional level.

Suppose now that it is difficult or impossible to devise an index of standards, or that available indexes are ambiguous. What should one expect to observe? If co-ordination costs are 'low' enough, the constituent assembly will assign the same function to two or more jurisdictional levels; that is, we expect concurrent authority.

Concurrent authority means that some kind of machinery will be set up to allow both levels of government to work together on devising and implementing the policies that are encompassed by the function assigned to both levels of government. Consequently, the problem of devising a metric or an index to formulate a policy is not as acute and indeed can usually be neglected. Concurrent authority may raise the total amount of investment in co-ordination and in administration, but when it exists and is a decision by a cost-minimizing constituent assembly it must, on an over-all basis, be resource-saving.

We conclude by repeating that in this model both minimum standards and concurrent authority are institutions that exist to make it possible for society to economize on the use of scarce resources in the public sector. One need not appeal to other motives to justify their existence. Contrary to a prevalent view, neither minimum standards nor concurrent authority necessarily implies a departure from an efficient use of resources.

Optimal distribution of the population
We may end this chapter by asking a different kind of question from the ones which have retained our attention until now, but one whose answer does shed additional light on the least-cost model by showing how it relates to some recent work that deals with some aspect of the theory of the structure of the public sector.

In the foregoing discussion, we have assumed that in seeking to minimize the flow of resources allocated to organizational activities, the constituent assembly could, as it were, operate on two levels; it could change the assignment of functions, and / or it could redesign the boundaries of the jurisdictional map. We could have formulated a different problem. We could, for example, have taken the assignment of functions and the boundaries of jurisdictions and of jurisdictional levels as given and have required that the constituent assembly minimize the use of scarce resources used up in public sector organization by changing the distribution of the population between jurisdictions.

It is possible to argue that this is essentially the question which has been discussed recently in the literature and to which Flatters, Henderson, and Mieszkowski have given – albeit in a different framework (one in which organizational costs are neglected) – a definitive answer.[18] Their answer is indeed the correct one, given their frame of reference and their assumptions. One important limitation of their analysis, however, originates in the fact that they deal with a world in which only one tax base and one function exist.

We would argue that in a least-cost model the optimal distribution of the population must be determined by reference to assumptions about the relationship between changes in signalling, co-ordination, and administration and changes in the distribution of the population, and that given the market rate of interest, citizens should be jurisdictionally located in such a way as to ensure that the internal rate of return on each kind of organizational investment be equal to that rate of interest. Departures from this optimal situation, due to capital market imperfections or to externalities in the organizational activities, could then be remedied by a selective use of Pigovian taxes and subsidies along the lines indicated by Flatters, Henderson, and Mieszkowski.

18 F. Flatters, V. Henderson, and P. Mieszkowski, 'Public Goods, Efficiency, and Regional Fiscal Equalization,' *Journal of Public Economics* III 2 (May 1974) 99-112

We possibly should have paid more attention to this problem. But the formal similarity between a redistribution of the population and a reassignment of functions, or a redesigning of jurisdictional boundaries, means that the least-cost model could be applied to the problem of the optimal distribution of the population, if one so desired. It also means that our conclusions apply *mutatis mutandis* to the problem of the optimal distribution of the population.

5 MISASSIGNMENT OF FUNCTIONS

We cannot hope in a single section to analyse in detail all the various ways in which misassignment of functions may arise. It is sufficient to indicate that such a phenomenon can arise, point to some of its causes, and state how the problem can be resolved.

Functions are misassigned when citizens and governments have to use up more resources in mobility, signalling, administration, and / or co-ordination than they would in the least-cost outcome. It should be emphasized that if the constituent assembly does not move towards the equilibrium assignment table (Ω^*), because to do so would use up more resources in the use of reassignment instruments than would be gained, we do *not* have misassignment of functions; we have an equilibrium. A misassignment arises only when net gains in resources are not captured. How can this happen?

Functions can be misassigned because of imperfection in the capital market, which prevents equality of the various internal rates of return with each other and with the market rate of interest. Suppose, to illustrate with one example, that $\rho_{H_E} > i$, while $\rho_{H_Z} = \rho_{H_A} = i$, that is, that the internal rate of return on investment in co-ordination is larger than the market rate of interest, because of the existence of some capital market imperfection. Co-ordination services will be provided in smaller amount than would be the case if such an imperfection would not exist.

If we hold to the assumption made in Section 3 above, that investment in co-ordination relative to that in administration falls as γ increases, a reduction in co-ordination will flatten out the H^G curve of Figure 7.4 – downwards. Since the dH^C curve will remain unchanged, the equilibrium value of γ will rise, that is, the constituent assembly will assign some functions to a higher level of government than it would otherwise. That is what we mean by a misassignment of functions.

If, to change the example, the imperfections in the capital market were such as to lead to a situation where $\rho_{H_A} > i$, while $\rho_{H_Z} = \rho_{H_E} = i$, then the constituent assembly would be induced to assign some function at lower levels of government that it would otherwise assign higher up. The excessive decentralization that would result is a misassignment of functions.

The second general class of reasons for misassignment is the presence of external effects and economies of scale in the various organizational activities of the public sector. Suppose, again to illustrate that mobility is subject to economies of scale and / or to externalities, in such a way that its private rate of return is lower than its social internal rate of return. If, again, we stay with the assumption of Section 3 that the ratio of investment in mobility to that in signalling falls as γ increases, the H^C curve of Figure 7.3 will become steeper, and its marginal in Figure 7.4 will shift upwards. Given that the position of the dH^G curve will remain unchanged, the equilibrium value of γ will be higher than it would be in the absence of economies of scale in mobility.

What has to be emphasized at this point is that interjurisdictional spill-overs and externalities, the degree of 'publicness' of public-good type policies, and economies of scale in production and procurement, what we have called interactions and interdependencies, do *not* lead to a misassignment of functions. The various organizational activities of the public sector exist to deal with these non-market interactions and as a consequence they cannot themselves lead to misassignment. It is only 'non-market interaction' in the organization of the public sector itself that can lead to misassignment.

As a final point, note that levies and grants evaluated in Pigovian fashion and paid as intergovernmental grants could lead to the internalization of organizational externalities and economies of scale and therefore to an optimal assignment of functions in the least-cost model. Intergovernmental grants in this case would be paid to eliminate underinvestment in organizational activities, that is, to induce more investment of time and other resources in certain aspects of the public sector and eliminate over-investment in other opportunities. Though the object of attention is different than in the traditional theory of externality, the theory itself applies without difficulty. Efficiency would again require that these grants be conditional.

8
Representative government models of federalism

1 INTRODUCTION

In previous chapters we emphasized that one of the characteristics of least-cost models was that members of the constituent assembly, and therefore the assembly itself, had no preferences of their own about the assignment table.[1] In making a decision about assignments, the constituent assembly simply calculated the costs of the various organizational activities engaged in by citizens and governments and selected the one for which these costs were a minimum. It was governed solely by these considerations.

If one departs from the assumption that organizational resource costs are minimized by the constituent assembly it is easy to assume that members of the assembly have preferences of their own for particular assignments. Furthermore, it must follow that if these preferences are satisfied, more resources will be used by citizens and by governments for organizational purposes than in the least-cost outcome. The difference between the cost of organizational activities when the preference for a particular assignment on the part of the constituent assembly is satisfied and the least-cost outcome defined in the previous chapter, therefore, is the organizational cost of satisfying these preferences.

It must be noted immediately that the organizational resource costs of satisfying a preference for a particular assignment, which for simplicity we may call excess organizational costs, are not borne by the members of the constituent assembly. The excess costs of signalling and mobility are borne directly by citizens *qua*

1 It might have been more in conformity with current usage to call this chapter 'Public Choice Models of Federalism.' However, since this last term seems to be used more and more to describe political party competition and median voter models, both of which appear to us to be of limited interest and largely removed from political reality, we have opted for a different nomenclature.

citizens, and those of administration and co-ordination are borne by citizens in their role as taxpayers. It is only as citizens and taxpayers that members of the constituent assembly partake in the extra costs of meeting their preference for particular assignments.

In Chapter 6 we recognized the possibility of two different kinds of constituent assemblies which we called uni-level and multi-level assemblies. The first, it will be recalled, designated assemblies composed of *constituants* coming from only one jurisdictional level of government, and the second, assemblies made up of *constituants* from two or more levels.

To proceed with the discussion of the present chapter, we describe in the next section the forces at play in uni-level assemblies first when there are no bureaucrats in the picture and then when they play a role. The only reason for discussing assignment problems in the absence of bureaucrats in a representative government model is to simplify the exposition: it makes it easier to discover the meaning of certain assumptions. Then in Section 3, we discuss the working of multi-level assemblies in which the *constituants* have different preferences about assignments. In Section 4, we examine the effects of introducing the reassignment instruments in the picture. We conclude by indicating that representative government models of federalism presented in this chapter are in all likelihood only a subgroup of all possible models of that kind.

2 UNI-LEVEL ASSEMBLIES

Uni-level constituent assemblies, as just pointed out, are composed of the politicians which are elected at one level of government. They are not usually elected to serve exclusively as *constituants*, but make decisions about the assignment of functions as well as about policies. To put it differently, governing politicians at one level of government sometimes act as legislators deciding on policies and sometimes as *constituants* making decisions about assignments.

It therefore seems reasonable to assume that the same considerations will govern these politicians both in their role as legislators and in that as *constituants*. To be specific, we assume that each politician can be represented by a utility function defined not only over public policies, but also over all possible assignment tables, and that they seek to maximize this function subject to technological and institutional constraints.

Among the technological constraints, one must include the production or procurement procedures that are imposed by nature and the state of the arts. Also included are the reassignment instruments used to alter the assignment table which we discussed in Chapter 6. The institutional constraints comprise the critical value of the re-election variable below which a governing party is defeated, and the re-election function which indicates how and in relation to what variables the probability of re-election varies.

Formally the new problem (a variant of the one examined in Chapter 5) is to maximize[2]

$$U^p = U^p(S_k, \Omega_i, e_i) \tag{8.1}$$

subject to

$$S_k = S_k(L_k, K_k), \tag{8.2}$$

$$\Omega_i = \Omega_i(y_i) \tag{8.3}$$

$$ii^p \geq ii^{p*} \tag{8.4}$$

and

$$ii^p = ii^p(S_k, \Omega_i, e_i, c), \tag{8.5}$$

where U^p is the utility derived by politician p; S_k is a particular public policy; L_k and K_k are labour and capital used to produce or procure S_k; Ω_i are assignment tables; y_i are the reassignment instruments; e_i are amenities of office additional to political power and include such things as statesmanship, common good, place in history, leisure, private wealth, and personal prestige; ii^p is the probability of re-election variable; ii^{p*} is the critical value of that variable, below which a party is defeated; and c is the degree of political competition between political parties.

The extent to which politicians can seek the amenities of power (e_i) or can implement policies (S_k) which are different from those desired by the citizenry, and / or the extent to which they can impose assignments (Ω_i) which are at variance from those preferred by citizens depends critically on the size of ii^p relative to ii^{p*}. The larger the difference $(ii^p - ii^{p*})$, the greater the degrees of freedom of politicians to pursue their own preferences for S_k, Ω_i, and e_i and to neglect those of the citizenry.

It is therefore important to know what are the factors that help determine the value of both these variables. We begin by ii^{p*}. As one of us has already argued,[3] ii^{p*} depends on the characteristics of the decision rules that are operative in a given society, that is on the rules of representation and of the formation of government (variously called cabinet, executive, administration, etc.) and on the

2 Since Ω enters the re-election function (8.5), it is clear that this formulation of the problem assumes that citizens themselves have preferences between values of Ω; otherwise π could not vary with Ω.

3 A. Breton, *The Economic Theory of Representative Government* (Chicago: Aldine Publishing Co. 1974)

length and flexibility of the election period, that is, of the period between one election and another.

The value of ii^P will change, as indicated in equation (8.5) when S_k, Ω_i, e_i, and / or c change. For the sake of the present discussion, let us hold all these variables, except Ω_i, constant, and ask how ii^P varies when Ω_i (or γ_i) varies, or in other words, let us ask what is the effect of a change in the assignment table or centralization co-efficient on the probability of re-election variable.

The answer to this question is to be found in the fact that assignment tables are in the nature of pure public goods, in that the one that obtains at a moment in time governs the assignment of powers for every citizen in society. It follows that in general, that is, in a society in which citizens differ from each other, either because tastes, incomes, or both are different, ii^P may either rise or fall when γ rises depending on the distribution of preferences for γ. Only in simplified and essentially uninteresting models in which everyone is assumed to be identical will it be possible to give an unambiguous sign to the partial derivative of ii^P with respect to γ.[4]

However, even if the partial derivative cannot always be unambiguously signed, the governing party acting as a uni-level constituent assembly will, in general, choose an assignment table that differs from the least-cost assignment of the last chapter, and thus impose excess organizational costs on citizens. There are essentially three reasons for this. First, by choosing a value of γ that differs from γ^*, it may simply be satisfying the preferences of a subgroup of citizens for a more centralized or for a more decentralized federation, and thereby increasing the probability of its re-election.

To put it differently, consider the case where there exists a group of citizens which has a definite preference for a more decentralized public sector structure. We need not, of course, investigate the origin and nature of that preference, except to assume that it is one that would not be satisfied in the least-cost outcome. That group may be made up of citizens who are ideological Jeffersonians believing that a more decentralized structure possesses merits of its own, such as to be more conducive to the virtuous development of the citizenry. Changing the assignment table in the direction desired by that group will increase the probability of re-election of the governing party as constituent assembly, if the group is sufficiently large.

Second, a value of γ different from the least-cost γ^* may be chosen if there exist citizens who, even if they have no definite preference for a particular level of centralization, can in a more centralized or in a more decentralized structure

4 Exactly the same argument can be made with respect to a large class of public policies. See *ibid*.

shift the burden of organizational costs – or even of the cost of public policies (S_k) – to other citizens in society. For example, suppose that in a decentralized sector, the more efficient alternative opened to coerced citizens would be to move and thus to incur moving costs, whereas in a more centralized structure they could rely on signalling already engaged in by another group of citizens. These individuals would favour the centralization because it would enable them to become free riders on the other groups' investment in signalling. If the politicians as *constituants* need the support of these citizens, they will move towards a more centralized federal structure.

Third, excess organizational costs may be imposed on the citizenry or on subgroups of the citizenry by a governing party as constituent assembly which chooses to use up some of its available degrees of freedom to satisfy a preference of its own for a particular assignment, even if that preference is at variance with those of the citizenry.

So far we have worked with a model of a constituent assembly in which politicians, but not bureaucrats, have a role to play. In that simplified world, it has not been possible to isolate any particular force that would allow us to predict a long-term tendency of federal structures to become more centralized or more decentralized. The outcomes of this simplified representative government model depend on the preferences of the citizenry, on the distribution of these preferences, on the preferences of elected governing representatives, on the distribution of organizational and public policy costs over citizens, or on all of these. In the absence of empirical knowledge, not only about these preferences and distributions, but also about how they tend to evolve through time, it is not possible to identify long-run tendencies.

The situation, however, is altered when we move from this simplified model to one that is slightly more complex, in that, in addition to politicians, it allows for the presence of bureaucrats in the decision-making process. The hypothesis, already introduced in Chapter 5, which we may restate here, adapting it to the present context, is that bureaucrats maximize utility functions defined over public policies (S_k), but also assignment tables (Ω_i), subject to rules, regulations, and procedures which need not retain out attention in this chapter.[5] We argued in Chapter 5 that the value of S_k and of Ω_i which makes utility as large as possible for bureaucrats is also the one which makes bureaucratic power a maximum. We finally argued that under certain simplifying assumptions maximum power could be approximated by maximum budget. We will work with these simplifications

5 For a detailed analysis of the effect of alternative rules and procedures on the behaviour of bureaucrats, see R. Wintrobe, 'The Economics of Bureaucracy' (unpublished Ph D dissertation, University of Toronto 1975).

in what follows. To them we add a further simplification: we assume throughout the remainder of this chapter, that, except for the administration and co-ordination component, the size of the budget of all governments at all jurisdictional levels is held constant. In other words, expenditures on public policies by all governments are not allowed to vary; only the expenditures on administration and co-ordination can change.

Before we are in a position to use the above hypothesis concerning the behaviour of bureaucrats, we must focus on two of the four components of organizational costs, that is, on administration and co-ordination costs. The reader will recall that these two types of costs exhaust the total of organization costs on the governmental side of the public sector, which we have consistently distinguished from the citizens' side.

Administration and co-ordination, we need not insist, are paid by taxpaying citizens. To put it differently, though it is true that these two kinds of costs are governmental costs, they have to be paid by taxpayers – which, of course, includes politicians and bureaucrats. We now note that administration and co-ordination costs paid by taxpaying citizens add to the budgets of bureaus and that a fraction of these budgets accrues as income to bureaucrats.

In uni-level constituent assemblies in which both politicians and bureaucrats have a role to play, the bureaucrats will have a preference and seek to achieve assignment tables that make expenditures by taxpaying citizens on administration and co-ordination as large as possible. In this way they will maximize the size of their budgets, and hence their power and utility. We may now ask, first, whether a federation will become more centralized or more decentralized if bureaucrats are successful, and, second, under what conditions they will be successful in satisfying their preference for particular assignments.

To illustrate the nature of the answer to the first question, consider two different functions only, namely f_1 and f_2. Assume that when f_1 is centralized, administration expenditures by taxpayers and hence receipts by bureaucrats at the jurisdictional level at which the uni-level assembly is located are equal to $100, while when it is decentralized expenditures on co-ordination with lower levels are $200. Assume further that when f_2 is centralized, administration expenditures are equal to $300.00, when decentralized $150. In these circumstances, budget maximizing bureaucrats will support decentralization of f_1 and centralization of f_2, since that will generate a co-ordination and administration budget of $500, while centralization of both functions would generate $400, decentralization $350, and centralization of f_1 and decentralization of f_2 only $250.

The reader will recall that in Chapter 7 we assumed that co-ordination activities and co-ordination costs increase as the public sector becomes more decentralized. If we still hold to this assumption, it must follow that in general bureaucrats will support the centralization of those functions for which expenditure on administration is larger when centralization is highest than expenditure on co-ordination when centralization is lowest.

We turn now to the second question, whether bureaucrats working for uni-level constituent assemblies are likely to obtain what they support. The answer must depend first on the size of the excess organizational costs which satisfying these preferences entails and therefore on the loss in degrees of freedom which such a change would inflict on the governing party as constituent assembly; and second, on whether the governing party wants to use up excess degrees of freedom in that way, a desire that surely depends on the congruence or dissonance of the preferences of politicians with those of bureaucrats.

Given that politicians often have excess degrees of freedom, it seems reasonable that they would sometimes accede to the wishes of their bureaucrats; therefore one would observe a tendency towards centralization in the direction of the jurisdictional level at which the governing party as constituent assembly is located for every function for which administration exceed co-ordination costs at a high level of centralization. This may be the explanation for the alleged tendency to centralization towards provincial and state levels – which are all uni-level assemblies – in many countries.

3 MULTI-LEVEL ASSEMBLIES

In multi-level constituent assemblies the *constituants* come from at least two different jurisdictional levels. Whereas in uni-level cases junior or subordinate jurisdictional levels are creatures of senior governments and are given existence and assigned powers by them acting as constituent assemblies, junior governments act as parties to assignment decisions in multi-level cases.

The setting of assignment decisions is therefore a more complex one. The hypotheses we make about the actors – politicians acting as *constituants*, and bureaucrats – are the same as for uni-level assemblies, so that the setting is one where politicians from different jurisdictional levels – all elected representatives – meet to make decisions about the assignment table that will maximize their own utilities. Similarly, bureaucrats come from different jurisdictional levels and each one seeks for his level those powers that will make his budget (and his power) as large as possible.

In this setting, which is essentially one of bargaining and negotiation, are there precise outcomes or predictions to which one can point, besides the obvious and not very interesting one that everything depends on the relative strengths of the participants? To put it in a different way, in a model in which the objectives of the various participants will not, in general, converge in a given direction, will the outcome always be *a priori* indeterminate, or will forces impart some predictability to the results?

To derive definite predictions, we assume that the *constituants* in multi-level assemblies engage in trades in which powers or functions are sold, loaned, rented, or subdivided. The trades we have in mind involve the sale of a function for a sum of money, or the loan of a function for a period of time for a sum of money. We do not have surrogate trades in mind, but *bona fide* exchanges of money for functions between the members coming from different jurisdictional levels. Even if it is true that an outside observer would witness trades of money for functions, the purpose of the exchanges is to improve the level of utility of all parties, by altering, in the desired direction, the probability of re-election for politicians and the degree of power or size of budget for bureaucrats.

Should one expect *constituants* from one jurisdictional level to enter negotiations more often as buyers of functions or as sellers, or should one expect all participants to be sometimes buyers and sometimes sellers? We conjecture that *ceteris paribus, constituants* at the level which has, at some time in the past, been assigned the more productive tax bases – the tax bases which are the more elastic as well as those which are less 'mobile' – will enter negotiations as purchasers of functions. Simply the one with the most revenue will be the buyer.

Whether a trade will be effected or not depends on factors which are essentially those discussed in the previous section. To see how they work in the present context, assume, to simplify, that the 'initial' assignment is the least-cost assignment, and that the more productive tax bases have been assigned to the federal jurisdictional level. Assume also that when the multi-level assembly meets, the *constituants* at the federal level enter as buyers of a function which in the least-cost assignment had been given to the provincial level. Under these circumstances, will a trade be effected knowing that if the trade takes place excess organizational costs will be imposed on the citizenry? To answer this question, suppose that the citizenry is satisfied with the least-cost assignment so that the excess organizational costs will reduce the support which it will give to the governments involved.

Focussing first on politicians as *constituants* and disregarding their bureaucrats for the moment, we predict that trade will take place between them for any of the following reasons: (1) politicians have excess degrees of freedom and choose to spend some of them to satisfy a preference for more centralization; (2) politicians have excess degrees of freedom and choose to spend some of them to achieve other objectives such as appeasing their bureaucrats or making a reputation as statesmen, even though they have themselves no preference for more centralization; (3) politicians seek to obtain by such trades more degrees of freedom. (For example, when a function is transferred to a higher level of government, junior governments not having to make any policy decisions with respect to that function may gain the support of some citizens who would otherwise have opposed them.)

If for any of the above reasons trade takes place, it follows from our conjecture that the level to which the more productive tax base will have been assigned enters as buyer, that functions will have a tendency to move to that level. If, as is often the case and as we postulated above, that level is the senior level, one would predict a tendency of inter-level trades to lead to more centralization.

Turning now to bureaucrats, we should expect a tendency for both federal and provincial bureaucrats to prefer more centralization. In this case the reason is that the process of buying and of renting functions as well as that of subdividing them is one which involves not only a redistribution of expenditures between the two levels engaging in the trade, but also, more significantly, an increase in administration and co-ordination components of the budget at both levels. Indeed, assuming again that the federal level has been assigned the more productive tax bases, buying and renting functions imply transfers of money on policies implemented under other powers, while subdividing functions require transfers for the implementation of policies under the same powers. In both cases, consequently, trades will enhance the budget and presumably the power of bureaucrats at both levels.

Under the circumstances we have defined all bureaucrats will favour more centralization. The final outcome will therefore depend on whether politicians have excess degrees of freedom, and on whether they choose to spend some of them on satisfying their own preferences, if any, and those of their bureaucrats. That outcome is essentially uncertain. One suspects, at least, that when politicians have excess degrees of freedom, they will choose to use some of these to satisfy the centralizing preferences of their bureaucrats.

Moreover, if we still hold to the conjecture that the senior level enters as a buyer of functions and therefore as a party to trades that lead to more centralization, and, given that bureaucrats at all levels favour more centralization, changes in the degree of centralization will depend on the behaviour of politicians at junior levels.

The strength of the conclusion above, which depends on the assumption that the higher jurisdictional level has the more productive tax bases, can be tested by examining states where such tax bases have initially been assigned to lower levels. Everything said above should hold in reverse.

The reader should note that these trades, which lead to transfers, provide one explanation for interjurisdictional grants. We return to these grants in Chapter 12. A point that needs to be made here is that if the more productive tax bases are predominantly located at one level, there will generally be a tendency in a federal structure for these grants to exist. They are the outcome of trades between *constituants*.

4 INTRODUCING REASSIGNMENT INSTRUMENTS

So far we have discussed the assignment problem for the two separate cases of uni- and multi-level assemblies without saying a word about the reassignment instruments illustrated in Chapter 6. We have, in other words, assumed that the *constituants* were not constrained by specified procedure, or *a priori* rules in negotiation and bargaining or in making unilateral decisions about assignments.

We must now recognize that reassignment instruments constrain the behaviour of *constituants*. To illustrate the operation of these constraints, and remembering that it is costly to use them, we examine three separate ways in which the costs of the instruments have a determining influence on how *constituants* alter the assignment table.

The first of these is the size of the centralization co-efficient (γ) itself. We assume that when γ is larger, the number of jurisdictional levels (δ) that constitute a federation is relatively small and that when γ is smaller δ is relatively large. To put it differently, when a federation is highly centralized δ is relatively small and when it is decentralized δ is relatively large. Given this, we assume that when δ is large, the total cost (W) of using the reassignment instruments (y_i) is also large; while when δ is small, W is lower.

This would mean that the cost of changing the assignment table would, *ceteris paribus* (ie, when the other two factors to be described below are held constant), be larger in the United States and Canada than in France or the UK. This is not an empty conclusion as we shall discover shortly, and we justify making it on the ground that when there are more jurisdictional levels, multi-level assemblies are more likely to exist, and the costs of implementing and enforcing a decision, in addition to those of reaching one, are higher.

Second, we assume that the level of W varies according to whether or not the constituent assembly is a uni- or a multi-level assembly and we postulate that in the first case the cost of using the y_i's are smaller than in the second, mostly because in the second a larger variety of preferences is represented in the decision-making body.

This second assumption implies that the cost of changing the assignment table will be larger in a country such as Canada where the constituent assembly is usually made up of federal and provincial representatives, than it would be in countries such as Italy or the United Kingdom or in the provinces of Canada, where the preferences of regions or local governments or municipalities are seldom, if ever, represented in the decisions. In countries like the United States or Switzerland the outcome should be very much as in Canada.

Finally, we assume that the cost of using the various y_i's will be higher if the assignment table is totally or partly entrenched in a constitutional document. This assumption needs no defence; it is obvious.

To illustrate the meaning of these three assumptions, we could compare two countries in which the centralization co-efficients depart from some least-cost value, or some value established on the assumption that the cost of using the y_i's are zero, or some other arbitrary value, but opposite in direction, and in which both citizens and governments are moved by the same kind of forces. In such a context and given the assumptions above, we would have to conclude that the existing assignment would be altered less *ceteris paribus*[6] in the country with the largest number of jurisdictional levels where the make-up of the constituent assembly required multilateral bargaining between the representatives of many levels, or in which the assignment table was entrenched in a constitutional document or both. In more formal terms, this prediction states that if some $\gamma^0 < \gamma^*$ (where γ^* is a γ derived assuming $y_i = 0$, for example) there will be less tendency to move to γ^* than if $\gamma^0 > \gamma^*$.

5 CONCLUSION

The models we have suggested above do not have the definiteness of those developed in Chapter 7. That is because the assumptions used in the present chapter do not have the same strength and simplicity as those underlying the least-cost models. This may not be a major drawback. The final test, of course, is to be found in our capacity to understand the forces operating in federal states. For this reason, we do not like to put the least-cost and the representative government models – which are built on many of the same building blocks – in opposition to each other, but prefer to use all of them to model different aspects of federal structures.

Furthermore, we wish to note that the domain of representative government models is much broader than that of least-cost models as we have conceived them, and that for at least two reasons. First, bureaucrats play no autonomous role nor can they ever play any role to alter decisions in the least-cost models. That again makes for definiteness, but eliminates much richness. Since the modelling of bureaucratic behaviour is still in its early stages the development of these models will affect the results of the representative government models derived above. Second, the range of alternative hypotheses about individuals, and about such

6 A *ceteris paribus* that incorporates the elements discussed in Sections 2 and 3.

things as the distribution of functions, which the representative governments models will allow, is much broader than that of the least-cost models. For these reasons we believe that, much more than the least-cost models, the representative-government models have potential as analytical devices for the study of both the special characteristics and the evolution of federal states.

It is, however, easy to exaggerate the differences between these two types of models, especially with respect to the predictions to which they lead. Indeed, if the institutional structure is such that governing parties must, to remain in office, meet the preferences for public policies of a large number of citizens, then a representative government type constituent assembly will in the long run tend towards an assignment of powers identical to that produced by a least-cost assembly. This follows from the simple fact that politicians are elected by citizens and that citizens who ultimately must carry the burden of both their own and the governmental organizational costs will favour those parties which make these costs as small as possible.

PART THREE
SPECIAL TOPICS

9

The selection of topics

The chapters in Part Two are of general application. It is possible, however, that some of our readers – especially those trained as economists – may have read those chapters as if they applied exclusively to the assignment of supply functions, but not to the assignment of such other functions as regulation, revenue, redistribution, and stabilization. It is our purpose in Chapters 10 and 11 to discuss the application of our assignment theory to redistribution and stabilization and in Chapter 12 to assemble in one place our conclusions about interjurisdictional grants.

In one sentence, we chose to devote separate chapters to the assignment of redistribution and of stabilization because these have already been examined both in scholarly literature on public finance and in more polemical writings and because strong views, often at variance with those emerging from our models, are held by many students of public-sector structures. In the next two chapters we test the generality of our approach and compare it with the few positive predictions and the numerous normative prescriptions that appear in the existing literature. Ideally, we should also make the same comparisons in chapters on the regulatory and revenue functions, but the existing literature does not contain views that are explicit enough to warrant such an exercise. Instead, in the following pages, we limit ourselves to a brief summary of the more relevant writing on the assignment of revenue functions and of regulatory powers. Our brevity does not necessarily imply disagreement with the authors of the views mentioned. There is an important difference between our goals. Their recommendations about assignment are not based on a view of the total assignment problem, but simply on the best way of dealing *ad hoc* with some current question of tax policy. That our models sometimes suggest the same assignment as they recommend neither confirms nor refutes our approaches.

2 REVENUE FUNCTIONS

We turn first to the assignment of revenue functions. There is a voluminous literature on this subject, both official and academic. But the analysis of the assignment or reassignment of a specific tax base, frequently referring to its political and regional effects, and sometimes to its locational or trade impact, usually does not deal with the benefits or costs of alternative assignments.

However, we have found four questions that turn up in the many authors' analyses. These often imply an awareness of the importance of some component of organizational costs, but rarely is the analysis carried far enough to allow for the differential variability of organizational costs with respect to changes in the level to which a tax base is assigned.

For example, concern is often expressed about the heavy collection and other bureaucratic activities required to administer some tax. It is asserted that its collection costs and vulnerability to political criticism (perhaps as a 'nuisance' tax) are high relative to the revenue obtained. Enforcement and monitoring (administration activities) is said to be unduly costly not only for such minor tax bases as the excise tax on cheques or the stamp tax on notes, but also for such a major revenue base as manufacturers' sales tax in Canada. Furthermore, with reference to the assignment problem it is sometimes asserted that these taxes would be less costly to administer if they were levied by another jurisdictional level. Unfortunately, because this suggestion has not been followed up, it provides no basis for comparison with our own approach.

A second aspect of tax assignment is the cost of taxpayer compliance, and the distortions emerging from taxpayer response. There is concern that a particular base may be so heavily taxed, relative to alternative tax bases, that taxpayer adjustment and avoidance not only diminish revenues, but also seriously distort production and marketing in the private sector. Examples that are often suggested are provincial and state corporation sales and property taxes.

Once again, however, the literature on this source of concern does not come to grips with the general problem of the assignment of tax bases. At one level of discourse, evasion and avoidance of the corporation tax at lower jurisdictional levels, for example, are discussed only in terms of the 'problems' involved for the tax collector: the costs of administration are to be reduced, but those of co-ordination, signalling, and mobility are ignored. At a more analytical level of discourse the point is made that where industrial location is footloose and labour and capital are mobile, taxpayers will tend to migrate in search of lower taxes.[1]

---

1 Some of these studies are the results of searches for new revenue sources in less developed countries. Noteworthy among these are N. Kaldor, *An Expenditure Tax* (London:

Conversely, where an industry's location is resource- or market-oriented, fear is expressed that more than one level of government will unfairly and inefficiently overtax them. Such devices as tax credits or tax deductibility as means of vertical co-ordination, and devices like treaties, credits, and explicit harmonization agreements as means of horizontal co-ordination are described and analysed. This literature is very detailed. Because it assumes that more co-ordination among jurisdictions would always be better than less, that is, because it implicitly assumes that the costs of co-ordination are zero, its treatment of the assignment problem is systematically biased towards excessive investment in co-ordination and in harmonization. Indeed, that literature is not so much concerned with the structure of government finance as with the distortions and incentives that some taxes create in the private sector of federal states.

Allen and Unwin 1965); R.M. Bird, *Taxation and Development: Lessons from Colombian Experience* (Cambridge, MA: Harvard University Press 1970); U.K. Hicks, *Federalism and Economic Growth in Underdeveloped Countries* (London: Allen and Unwin 1961) and *Development Finance, Planning and Control* (Oxford: Clarendon Press 1965). For a recent bibliography of studies mostly by American authors, and citations of earlier bibliographies, see O. Oldman and S. Surrey, 'Technical Assistance in Taxation in Developing Countries,' in R.M. Bird and J.G. Head, eds, *Modern Fiscal Issues: Essays in Honour of Carl S. Shoup* (Toronto: University of Toronto Press 1972) 278-91. Perhaps more relevant here is another set of studies dealing with the reform of whole tax systems. Among these are *Report on Japanese Taxation by the Shoup Commission,* 4 vols (Tokyo: General Headquarters, Supreme Commander, Allied Powers 1949); J.S.H. Hunter, *Revenue Sharing in the Federal Republic of Germany* (Canberra: Centre for Research on Federal Financial Relations, Australian National University 1973); The Redcliffe-Maud Report, *Report of the Royal Commission on Dominion-Provincial Relations* II, *Recommendations*, Sections B, Public Finance, C, Administrative Economies, and D, Dominion-Provincial Aspects of Transportation (Ottawa: King's Printer 1940), 175-219; R. Mathews, *Fiscal Federalism: Retrospect and Prospect* (Canberra: Centre for Research on Federal Financial Relations, Australian National University 1974); and G.J. Stigler, 'Tenable Range of Functions of Local Government,' in US Congress Joint Economic Committee, Subcommittee on Fiscal Policy, *Federal Expenditure Policy for Economic Growth and Stability* (Washington, DC: Government Printing Office 1957) 213-17. More specialized is a large literature on the municipal tax base. References to the work of J.R. Hicks and U.K. Hicks will be found in the works cited above.
    As examples of recent work, see the Graham Report, *Report of the Royal Commission on Education, Public Services and Provincial Municipal Relations* (Halifax: Queen's Printer 1974); and J.A. Maxwell, *Financing State and Local Governments*, rev. ed. (Washington, DC: Brookings Institution 1969). The publications of the US Advisory Commission on Intergovernmental Relations contain many investigations of the reassignment of tax bases. See, for example, the staff reports *Federal-State Coordination of Personal Income Taxes* (Washington, DC: ACIR, October 1965). For a recent survey, see L.L. Ecker-Racz, *The Politics and Economics of State-Local Finance* (Englewood Cliffs, NJ: Prentice-Hall 1970) 31-64 and 165-8.

A third question stems from the belief that jurisdictions that make, and depend on, federal grants and other such payments are encouraged to be 'fiscally irresponsible' in that governing parties do not, or need not, exercise the frugality in spending that would characterize the use of funds raised from their own citizens. We have examined the problem of fiscal irresponsibility in Chapter 7; here we note the effect of this question on the tax base assignment literature.

Concern about fiscal irresponsibility has led to the proposal that each level of government should be fiscally autonomous, a proposal also advanced by writers who, while not preoccupied with the irresponsibility problem, nevertheless regard fiscal autonomy as an end in itself. Autonomy (meaning freedom from the conditions and dependence attached to grants and payments from other jurisdictional levels) can be achieved, ideally, by assigning to each level its own separate tax bases. A second-best proposal in that literature is to assign to each jurisdictional level a fixed percentage share of a base that is taxable by more than one level.

Proposals like this make sense only if we can suppose that these authors believe that co-ordination costs are very high. Otherwise, the obvious alternative to revenue autonomy or fixed-ratio tax sharing would be to rely on co-ordination activities to prevent over- or under-utilization of a tax base that is jointly occupied by more than one jurisdictional level. Most writers implicitly dismiss the idea of such effective co-ordination. Consequently this literature is merely wistful – the authors are saying little more than that it would be a happy state of affairs if there were enough revenue bases to permit each jurisdictional level to possess its own and thus avoid the need for co-ordination.

The major exception to this point in the literature is to be found in the consensus that real property ought to be, and usually is, assigned to local jurisdictional levels. Such an assignment, in addition to meeting the alleged autonomy and responsibility goals mentioned in the preceding paragraphs, is said to have other advantages as well.[2] Among these is that the interjurisdictional incidence of property taxation is smaller than that of alternative tax bases. Another advantage is said to lie in the cyclical stability of real estate values which, it is argued, guarantees stability of revenues to local jurisdictions and hence their independence over the whole business cycle.[3] These generalizations about the assignment of the property tax though apparently quite definite are economically unsatisfactory

---

2 See Wallace E. Oates, *Fiscal Federalism* (New York: Harcourt Brace Jovanovich 1972) Chapter 4, 119-79; also A. Marshall, *Principles of Economics*, 8th edition (London: Macmillan 1930) Appendix G.
3 For a representative study with many references, see R.W. Rafuse, Jr, 'Cyclical Behavior of State-Local Finances,' in R.A. Musgrave, ed., *Essays in Fiscal Federalism* (Washington, DC: Brookings Institution 1965) 63-121.

because they totally neglect the real organizational costs of achieving the objectives of autonomy and fiscal responsibility.

A fourth question that one finds in the literature is whether private activities in each subsector of the economy ought to be taxed by the jurisdictional level that has responsibility for their regulation. Those who follow Tinbergen on the relationship between instruments and target variables favour the assignment at the same jurisdictional level of both regulatory authority and tax bases.[4] Legal arguments about constitutions appear to go in the same direction. In both approaches, for example, international trade and import duties, currency and seignorage, mineral leasing and royalties, airports and landing fees, highways and road taxes would be assigned to the same level.

Assignment problems arise because there are more types of regulation than there are complementary tax bases, so that a dispersion of regulatory functions among jurisdictional levels cannot easily be matched by a dispersion of suitable taxing powers. In terms of our own models, this disparity would be expected to lead to investment in co-ordination between the jurisdictions that tax and those that regulate. In the literature, however, because the cost of co-ordination is implicitly assumed to be prohibitively high, this interesting problem is not further investigated.

3 REGULATORY FUNCTIONS

Our distinction between regulatory and supply functions is unknown to constitutional law and therefore constitutions only list the subject over which powers are conferred. Similarly, public finance economists, to the extent they have addressed this subject, have failed to distinguish between them. However, the distinction is an important one. For example, it is easy to imagine that powers to provide a commodity such as railway transportation might be assigned to one jurisdictional level, while some power to regulate, ie, to set rates, to decide on destinations, schedules, and quality of service might be conferred on another. Indeed, the industrial organization literature often deals with the distinction and conflicts that may arise between the two types of powers.

Because, as just indicated, the literature does not provide any propositions with which we might compare the predictions of our models, we do not pursue

---

4 See J. Tinbergen, *On the Theory of Economic Policy* (Amsterdam: North-Holland 1952) Chapter 7. However, in his *Economic Policy: Principles and Design* (Amsterdam: North-Holland 1967), Chapters 5 and 8, Tinbergen goes into the problems of co-ordination between jurisdictions with different 'welfare functions,' and dismisses any simple argument for centralization of policy instruments. See also L. Johansen, *Public Economics* (Amsterdam: North-Holland 1971) Chapter 2.

the matter of the assignment of regulatory powers further in this book. We hope that by now, however, the reader will be convinced that our models, with their emphasis on organizational costs, provide the means of analysing the assignment of regulatory and supply functions separately.

4 CONCLUSION

The upshot of this chapter is that, although they would seem to offer scope for the critical application of our models, neither the level of assignment of revenue powers nor that of the assignment of regulatory powers has so far received enough analytical attention in the economic literature to allow for a comparison of conclusions. Hence we shall confine Part Three's chapters to three other subjects much more widely discussed and for which definite conclusions, against which we can measure our own, have been established: the assignment of powers with respect to redistribution and with respect to stabilization, and the question of inter-jurisdictional grants.

10

The assignment of
redistribution functions

1 INTRODUCTION

To ask which jurisdictional levels should redistribute is to invite the response that whichever governments have presided while market forces, inheritance, and routing public expenditures have shaped the existing distribution must be the logical candidates for reshaping it. In other words, each jurisdiction should have its own redistribution branch. This facile response evades the problem of assigning the redistribution functions, but it does suggest a need for interpreting what 'the assignment of redistribution' means. Two senses of this phrase may be suggested, one too abstract, the other perhaps too concrete.

In the first sense, the redistributive function depends on a jurisdiction's having not only responsibility, but also motive. Because, as the paragraph above suggests, any act of economic policy on any question involves the government that does it (or permits it) in a distributive choice, what must matter for the assignment of the redistribution function is not who should have the capacity, but who should have the will – or the motivation – to redistribute. When all can act, who should bear the responsibility?

We do not attempt to approach the assignment question in this way. To do so requires imagining, and depending on, an assignment model in which the constituent assembly (already a somewhat abstract conception) has the non-operational role of assigning states of mind – called will, or motivation – to some jurisdictional levels, and withholding from others the power to have these states of mind.

We shall avoid asking the reader to imagine the constituent assembly attempting this by interpreting the 'redistribution function' and its assignment in another more concrete sense. We shall define this function as the power to employ a particular instrument of redistribution: a system of income transfers, a tax base, or an in-kind social welfare benefit. This sense may seem a little restrictive. But focusing on a single instrument is broad enough to permit full recognition in what follows of an important characteristic of the assignment of this function. Purposive redistribution carried out by the use of the redistributive instruments may be assigned to more than one jurisdictional level so that the policies of one government either reverse or reinforce the redistributive effects of the policies of another. Furthermore, even the assignment of a particular redistributive instrument may be subdivided into more finely defined assignments, so that for example, a particular tax base can serve as the foundation for several governments' redistributive policies. If the reader wishes to ignore these subdivisions of the redistributive function, he must be prepared to find that it is apparently usually assigned concurrently to several levels. Our definition permits a simplified treatment of the concurrent authority phenomenon: the problem of the assignment of redistribution is narrowed to the choice of a jurisdictional level to make policies concerning one specific instrument.[1]

Using the second sense of definition of the redistribution function, this chapter's argument is constructed of four building blocks. The first of these is a theory of redistribution based on a notion of empathy. The second is a model of redistribution by 'taking' stemming from the general idea that decision rules allow governments to bias income distributions in favour of majorities. The third is a mobility model in which a citizen moving in search of lower taxes or higher transfers constrains the amount of redistribution undertaken by lower-level jurisdictions. The last is the set of assignment models of Chapters 7 and 8 in which citizen investment in moving and signalling and government investment in co-ordination and administration are the determinants of the jurisdictional level to which any function is assigned.

We briefly examine these in turn.

The first building block is the theory of income redistribution initially inspired by the development of the implications of interdependent utility functions by Vickrey, Boulding, and Hochman and Rodgers. It focuses on the conceptual problem of considering not only a flow of redistributional payments, but also a state

1 An advantage of our restriction of the scope of redistribution is that, by focusing on the assignment of a particular instrument, we can refer to recent debates on the assignment of particular powers, such as that in Canada about the assignment of family security responsibilities (1971) and that in the United States about the administration of the poverty program (1964). In these debates the participants spoke and wrote as though the issues were much broader than those actually in question. For earlier controversies, see A.H. Birch, *Federalism, Finance and Social Legislation in Canada, Australia and the United States* (Oxford: Clarendon Press 1955). The economics of US proposals since 1964 are referred to by the contributors to Wallace E. Oates, ed., *Financing the New Federalism* (Baltimore: Johns Hopkins University Press, for Resources for the Future, Inc. 1975).

of distribution as objects of public choice. In it citizens can be regarded as having preferences for combinations of income for themselves and for as many other persons as enter their utility functions. These preferences can be interpreted in two ways: as indicating their demand to change the difference between the income of some other persons and themselves, and so indicating their empathy with or envy of such persons; and as indicating their demand to change the entire social distribution of income, and so indicating their preferences for alternative distributions. We have found it convenient to think of the former as a demand for *partial* income redistribution, and the latter for *general* redistribution. The first may give rise either to private transfers or government-organized redistributions; the second is always a demand for a public good.[2]

This building block makes several contributions to our analysis of assignment. In the first place it demonstrates that government is necessary. Even a world of philanthropic, but individualistic, citizens would depend on government to implement their generosity. Voluntary action would not be adequate to bring about even small changes in the relative shares of social income enjoyed by various groups in society. To do this they need not only the right to give, but also access to the right to tax. Hence, if governments did not already exist, they would, for their redistributional functions alone, be invented.

In the second place, it suggests how we may interpret our model of the process of citizen investment in signalling and mobility when this model is applied to distributive policy. Citizens need not be pictured as simply supporting policies which will reduce their taxes or increase their transfer benefits; or (slightly more complexly) supporting some specific equalization measure, but no more. Instead, all citizens can be viewed as having preferences that vary from person to person in their inclusiveness and their intensity. By inclusiveness we mean the number of incomes, in addition to his own, that enter the preferences of each citizen. By intensity we refer to his strength of desire to add to or take from these incomes. (In a diagram, the former would be indicated by the number of dimensions on a preference function, and the latter by a marginal rate of substitution along contours of this function.) Inclusiveness can run from one, that is having concern only for one's own income, well towards infinity, that is having concern for everyone else's income (or having concern for the distribution of income among all

2 Lester C. Thurow, 'Income Distribution as a Public Good,' *Quarterly Journal of Economics* 85 (May 1971) 327-36; and H.M. Hochman, J.D. Rodgers, and Gordon Tullock, 'On the Income Distribution as a Public Good,' *Quarterly Journal of Economics* 97 (May 1973) 311-15; Yew-Kwang Ng, 'Income Distribution as a Peculiar Public Good,' *Public Finance* (1973) 1-9. For a suggestive definition of general redistribution, we refer the reader to the concept of non-revolutionary redistribution in K. Lancaster, 'Politically Feasible Income Redistribution in a Democracy,' *American Economist* XVII 2 (Fall 1973) 79-84.

persons in the world). Intensity can run from positive to negative feelings, from having an intense desire to share one's own income to wishing to acquire some of another person's. When policy does not produce a distribution that corresponds with their preferences, citizens are coerced and stimulated to invest in moving and in signalling; and governments to invest in co-ordination and administration.

The second building block is 'taking.' This term was coined by Richard Musgrave to describe the ability of a majority to pass legislation which, directly or indirectly, transfers a larger per capita fiscal benefit to itself than to the minority. An approach based on this capacity generates predictions that citizens will rely on voting power and decision rules to redistribute income favourably to themselves. Political life is viewed as a battle in which classes or parties attempt to 'take' from each other a larger share of the national income. Even in these circumstances the preference functions of those who would 'take' need not differ from the functions of the citizens who would give or would share. Behaviour that differs among identical citizens can be explained by whether a citizen belongs to a group whose income is likely to be augmented or diminished by proposed legislation.

The general approach to the assignment of redistribution in the literature of federal finance is a combination of the 'taking' view (the second building block) with a recognition of the effect of citizen mobility on redistribution by low-level governments (the third building block).[3] The combined approach of the two may be sketched as follows. If the power to redistribute were highly centralized, the political model summarized in the previous paragraph would lead to a certain degree of redistribution of income by the ruling party in favour of itself. The poor might, for example, legislate in favour of welfare policies; or the rich, if in control, might make it possible for extreme inequality to exist.

In a decentralized state, however, the majority and minority will be unevenly distributed among a number of provinces. Members of the national minority may become the ruling party in some provinces. In these provinces the redistribution may be opposite to that in others. Thus the tendency to redistribute may, over the whole society, be different from that in a unitary society. But that is not all. The third building block reminds us that many people are mobile. Those who belong to provincial minorities will have an incentive to move to provinces where their class or group is in control. The final amount of redistribution then

3 Elements of this approach will be found in the writings of many writers, although it should not be assumed that all disregard the concern for others mentioned as the first foundation. In addition to Wallace E. Oates, *Fiscal Federalism* (New York: Harcourt Brace Jovanovich 1972) 190-5 and Richard and Peggy Musgrave, *Public Finance in Theory and Practice* (New York: McGraw-Hill 1973) 21 and 606, see Mark V. Pauly, 'Income Redistribution as a Local Public Good,' *Journal of Public Economics* II 1 (April 1973) 35-58 and literature cited therein.

will depend not only on whether the 'rich' or the 'poor' are in an over-all majority, but also on how these are geographically distributed and who is able to move.

The fourth building block consists of our assignment models, applied to redistribution functions. As we have seen, when policy does not produce a distribution that corresponds with citizens' preferences they are induced to invest in mobility and signalling. Similarly, governments are stimulated to invest in administration and co-ordination activities. The amounts of investment in these four activities, varying with γ, influence any constituent assembly in its determination of the assignment of the power to use a redistributive instrument.

In the next two sections of this chapter we proceed to fit these four building blocks together in, first, a discussion of partial redistribution, and later, of general redistribution. One last assumption should, however, be made explicit: total income, and output, are assumed not to be reduced by the use of redistributive instruments. In other words, redistribution does not affect the amount available to be redistributed.

We do not believe that this particular assumption seriously restricts the generality of the chapter. Our reason is that most disincentive or deterrent effects of redistributive policies on supply, output, or income are invariant with respect to the level of government administering them. They are neither a result, nor a determinant, of the level to which redistributive powers have been assigned.

The chief exception to this assertion is already well known in the literature on federal finance. The level of redistribution policy does affect the location of economic activity and the movements of goods and factors. While we do not deny that this effect can impair the efficiency of the allocation of inputs, we wish to draw attention to the direct and indirect adjustments which it induces rather than to the mere fact of its existence. The 'distortion' of mobility and location, by changing both the level and the distribution of incomes, will stimulate citizens to invest in signalling and in further moving. These direct adjustments will in turn influence the constituent assembly in its determination of the degree of centralization, bringing about indirect adjustments in the form of different assignments of functions than if the distortions of location had not taken place.[4]

4 Put in other words, our goal is to predict the consequences for assignment of certain modes of redistribution. This goal requires us to trace the process by which assignment is adjusted. It does not require us to pause to praise (or condemn) either the distributional policies or their final consequence for γ. One of us has spilt much ink on that normative quest. See Anthony Scott, 'A Note on Grants in Federal Countries,' *Economica* XVII (1950) 416-22; J.M. Buchanan, 'Federal Grants and Resource Allocation,' *Journal of Political Economy* LX 6 (June 1952) 208-17; subsequent comments; Anthony Scott, 'The Economic Goals of Federal Finance,' *Public Finance* XIX 3 (1964) 241-88; and a later series of papers by Buchanan and others culminating in F. Flatters, V. Henderson, and P. Mieszkowski, 'Public Goods, Efficiency, and Regional Fiscal Equalization,' *Journal of Public Economics* III 2 (May 1974) 99-112.

2 PARTIAL REDISTRIBUTION

The assignment of partial redistribution policies to levels of government brings few new problems to light. The assignment models apply well. Citizen adjustment, government reaction, and organization activity are all, *mutatis mutandis*, as already discussed in Chapters 7 and 8.

Citizens may be assumed to desire the benefits of various redistribution policies for themselves and for those over whom their preference functions are defined. (Recent discussions in Canada and the United States have suggested that citizens may also have preferences about who should administer these policies, but we explicitly assume in this section that they have not.) For some citizens the amount of income received by (say) poor persons will exceed, or fall short, of the ideal distribution of income between rich and poor. The frustration generated by this excess or shortfall will cause investment of time and money in political participation by these citizens. Governments will also invest in administration and co-ordination activities, connected with the provision of a changed income for P. All these activities will vary with γ. Finally, these variations will influence the constituent assembly in its choice of the assignment of this redistributive responsibility.

In the following subsections we expand these ideas and speculate about the detailed reactions of citizens and governments to changes in the degree of centralization of partial redistribution policies.

Citizen adjustment

We first examine in more detail the reactions of citizens of a particular jurisdiction, J, to a particular redistribution proposal. The proposal is to tax those with incomes above a certain level and to transfer the revenue to citizens with lower incomes. (We might alternatively have chosen a proposal to pay for publicly provided services by means of a steeply progressive income tax.) Those who expect to pay will be said to belong to group R (rich); those who expect to receive to group P (poor). Members of group R will decide whether the net payment they must make, given the increase in the income of members of group P, increases or decreases their net welfare. Members of group P will do the reverse: decide whether the net transfer they will receive, given the fall in income of members of group R, increases or decreases their net welfare. If they are concerned about the incomes of members of the opposite groups, members of each group may either gain or lose net welfare from the introduction of the proposal; if they are not, members of R will lose and members of P will gain.

Investment in organization activity by members of the two groups will vary directly with their loss of net welfare. If the empathy of members of each group for members of the other group is weak, we would expect citizens R to invest in signalling to attempt to defeat the proposal and to plan to migrate away from jurisdiction J, or both. Citizens P will signal in support of the proposal, drop plans to emigrate, or both. (And citizens like R living elsewhere will drop plans to immigrate while citizens like P will plan to immigrate to jurisdiction J.)

On the other hand, if the empathy of members of each group for members of the other group is strong, the organization activity plans of members of the two groups will tend to be the reverse of that summarized above, at least so far as residents of J are concerned. Members of group R may be pleased and members of P distressed by the proposal and reveal these reactions in their signalling and moving activities.

Finally, if each group's members' empathy for members of the other group varies with their individual incomes, then members' incentives to invest in organizational activity will also vary. For example, the poorest members of each group might not share the satisfaction (or dissatisfaction) of wealthier group members with the proposed transfer scheme; they might even invest in signalling against a policy supported by the majority of their group.

The amount of investment in signalling depends on its cost to each person. In general, the authorities have argued that the cost of political participation (at least to the extent that it requires personal time and commitment) varies directly with a citizen's income.[5] If this is correct, we may combine it with the observations in the paragraph above to form a hypothesis as follows. A proposal to redistribute income in favour of the poor will be supported most vigorously by those with the lowest incomes and opposed most vigorously by the least wealthy of those who must pay for the transfer.

It is sometimes argued that redistributional proposals stimulate very vigorous signalling. The explanation offered is that governments cannot make transfers to one part of the citizenry without provoking opposition from the remainder. Transfers cannot benefit everyone; someone must pay. Indeed, everyone will signal, either for lower taxes or higher transfers.

This explanation disregards empathy. Those who must pay may approve of the proposed transfers and the necessary taxes. The task for government, when empathy is strong, may be merely to search for that transfer program that satisfies everyone. In less extreme situations, of course, redistribution may be as much a consequence of 'taking' as of empathy. As the amount of taking increases, signalling will increase. But, in general, the level of signalling about redistributive policies need not, dollar for dollar, be more than the level for other government activities.

5 See A. Downs, *An Economic Theory of Democracy* (New York: Harper and Row 1957) and A. Breton, *The Economic Theory of Representative Government* (Chicago: Aldine 1974).

What is the influence of centralization on the amount of signalling? Assume that moving is impossible. When γ is low, each small jurisdiction will have its own initial income distribution. Unless income groups are spread and mixed homogeneously across the jurisdictional map, a nation-wide minority group may find itself a ruling group in some places; in general, the political complexion of governments will vary and this will lead to interjurisdictional differences in redistributional policies. (An obvious expectation would be that in very poor regions there would be strong majorities favouring transfers to the poor, while in very rich regions support would be weaker.) Because, as we argued just above, unanimity on some transfer schemes is almost impossible, signalling on them would be intense. However, in spite of such possible differences in intensity, we see no reason to modify the argument of Part Two. We continue to expect that, as γ increases, the variance of the distribution of the preferences of citizens within each (increasingly larger) jurisdiction also increases, so that both the incentives for all persons to signal and the actual investment in signalling would rise.

The introduction of citizen moving complicates the above conclusions. Signalling and moving are to a certain extent substitutes, but moving is unlikely to be used alone. Even when redistributional policy is of great importance to a citizen, moving will be seen only as a final (and indivisible) type of organization activity. Only after the citizen has failed to obtain at home the policy he desires, may he decide, as second best, to take what is on offer somewhere else. Furthermore, the costs of moving, compared with those of voting, are probably greater so that most citizens will move out (or in) only after recourse to the ballot, and to other kinds of signalling activity as well, have been exhausted.

Nevertheless, we must devote special attention to mobility. We detect in the literature of federal finance a belief that, when redistribution policies are under debate, citizens will have a greater preference for investment in moving (rather than in signalling) than when other types of policy are being decided. We know of no research to support or refute this conjecture. But we can understand the prominence which moving plays in the literature and can suggest two possible explanations. In the first place, citizens may dislike the migratory consequences (such as an expected exodus of rich taxpayers or an influx of welfare recipients) of a redistribution policy more than its more immediate net effects. Indeed they may even welcome the latter and signal against it only because of their fear of the former effect. The threat of heavy migration, like an external diseconomy in the provision of redistributional services, may motivate citizens to signal against redistribution. Believing that such adverse signalling leads to under-provision of redistribution, observers have suggested that moving is the most important citizen organization activity.

There is a second explanation, touched on in an earlier paragraph, to explain the intensity of signalling against redistribution policies. It applies even better to moving. Because many supply and regulatory policies can come close to benefitting everyone, they may evoke neither passionate hostility nor warm enthusiasm. Those affected may take the trouble to vote, but invest in no other signalling or moving activity. In contrast, some redistribution policies, if empathy is not strong, will produce both winners and losers. Feelings of outrage, relief, or disappointment may be expressed. Citizens will increase their signal; more important, many will now move if there are greener fields elsewhere.[6]

How will mobility vary with the degree of centralization? The total amount of moving will be a positive function of the number of alternative policies (in other jurisdictions) that may attract a citizen dissatisfied with what his own government offers. It follows that when γ is low, and each small jurisdiction has its own redistribution policy, mobility will be high.[7] As γ increases, the reduction in the number of alternative redistributive policies will reduce investment in moving. The level of signalling, already high when γ is low (as discussed earlier) will tend to be even higher when each citizen faces the possibility that policies elsewhere will induce other citizens to migrate away or inwards.

Furthermore, each citizen's preferences (or standards) for domestic redistribution policies may become more demanding as he learns about policies elsewhere also resulting in higher signalling.[8] As γ increases, the need to signal in response to the threats and dangers of high mobility will decline and the rising variance among citizens' preferences in large γ jurisdictions will cause signalling to rise. On balance, the two effects on signalling may offset each other and signalling may remain constant, or not fall as much as mobility, when γ rises.

In sum, total citizen organization activity associated with redistributive poli-

6 In the literature, the migratory activity engendered by redistribution is itself sometimes offered as a determinant of the assignment of redistributive powers, especially in normative models. Compare the (opposite) arguments of the Musgraves in *Public Finance in Theory and Practice* 21-2, with those of J.M. Buchanan, 'Who Should Redistribute in a Federation?' Both authors appear to assume that citizens have little empathy for one another, and that all actual redistribution is 'taking' by majority voting.

7 This is not necessarily an equilibrium situation. As was discussed elsewhere in the present chapter, many small jurisdictions may be prevented by easy mobility from having distinct redistribution policies. Then the equilibrium amount of mobility may be very small even when γ is small.

8 This learning, or exemplary, phenomenon has not played a large role in our models of federalism, partly because it is more dynamic than the variables we think explain the equilibrium of centralization. Many political and some economic studies of federalism dwell on the learning, leadership, pilot project, or experimental possibilities for the economy of having examples that show the way to governments of other jurisdictions or levels. At one time the literature assigned this exemplary role to the central government, the provinces and cities learning from new central policies. Partial redistribution being a policy that all jurisdictional levels can provide at the same time, the exemplary role may be played for a given government by governments at the same level.

cies will probably fall as γ rises. But the changing mix of moving and signalling may prevent the total from falling more rapidly than for other functions, with respect to the degree of centralization. Thus the general analysis of investment by citizens (ie, H^C) in Part Two applies.

If H^C is higher, the difference stems from the propensity to move. In the absence of empathy, people may move to escape both unwanted redistribution policies and also other people. Such moving, or the threat of it, may stimulate more debate and more signalling than other kinds of policies. The assignment literature suggests that the high mobility of some citizens and its magnifying effect on the mobility and signalling of others is very significant for policy when γ is low. For its significance for the equilibrium value of γ, we must first examine government organization activities.

Government behaviour

Pursuing the application of the assignment model developed in Part Two, we now examine government organization activities associated with redistributional policy. These activities (including search, setting-up, operating, enforcement, and co-ordination activities) have often been omitted from recent discussions of the assignment of redistribution, thus permitting an exaggeration of the role of citizen activities. To be more specific, this omission appears to explain at least part of the belief that the individual incentive to invest in moving will not be moderated by a countervailing government activity. In turn, this belief has led to the conclusion that, when citizen mobility is not costly, redistribution must be assigned to senior jurisdictional levels.

Our general view is that our treatment of government organization activities in Part Two applies well to redistribution. Only three aspects of government administration and co-ordination require special comment at this stage.

The first comment is that, for each dollar redistributed by a government, investment in administration and co-ordination may well be higher than for an equal amount to spend on a supply policy. The chief reason for this is that governments must respond to citizens, and we have already argued that redistribution policies will stimulate more citizen moving than, and as much signalling as, the exercise of other functions.

Search activity, in particular, will display this higher level in response to citizen jumpiness about redistribution. Any governmental proposal about redistributive transfers or tax changes – indeed, any decision that there should be no changes – must be based on intense political homework, negotiation, and kit-flying. Politicians and their advisers seek indications not only of citizens' preferences about redistributional schemes and systems, but also of their trade-offs between these policies and complementary or compensatory policies under supply, regulatory, or stabilization powers. They invest in inquiries in search of new or better redistributive 'technology,' attractive or less threatening to doubtful or hostile voters.[9]

As for the effect of the changes in γ, the degree of centralization, we follow Chapter 7 in assuming that investment by governments in administration do not decrease (and may increase) as γ increases. The reasons for this assumption are given in that chapter. The larger the number of citizens in a jurisdiction, the more difficult it is to ascertain their preferences, demands, and thresholds of consent. Furthermore, the fewer the number of alternative jurisdictions to which dissatisfied citizens can migrate, the greater will be the demands on government for informed and discriminating response to signalling. As Pauly points out, even under complete centralization of redistribution, a national government could in principle do everything that local governments under extreme decentralization would have done.[10] But learning what different citizens will agree to, and making policies that differ across regional boundaries or other lines of distinctions between national citizens, will be costly.

The second comment concerns investment in co-ordination. All co-ordination is to be explained by the spill-overs or linkages between jurisdictions, but certain redistribution linkages are unique. In the first place, the utility interdependence or empathy that motivates much redistribution is no respecter of jurisdictional borders. Empathy, perhaps linking members of the same family, tribe, race, or religion, creates demands by citizens for policies that will lead to net transfers to those who are within their empathy span. And the required co-ordination activities do not initiate contacts between regions that are inadvertently connected by physical spill-overs; instead, they are needed to support and complement a tangle of personal and institutional 'trans-jurisdictional' bonds that flourish already.[11] Good examples are provided by the co-ordination activities that channel communications between a country of new settlement and its people's country of origin; between two jurisdictions whose people are unique in using the same language or having the same religion; or between jurisdictions that have until recently been united under one jurisdiction.[12]

---

9 Although at an earlier point in this chapter we assumed away concern about the disincentive effects of redistributive policies, we must point out here that politicians would also seek to satisfy voters that redistributive policies would not have such effects and would actively seek transfer systems that would justify such assurances.

10 Pauly, 'Income Redistribution as a Local Public Good' 41

11 For more on 'transnational' relations, see Robert S. Nye and others, *International Organization* XXVIII 4 (1976).

12 The linkages of empathy across jurisdictional boundaries often seem weak and temporary, depending on the memory of generations of people who once shared common citizenship. Pauly and others have remarked that the existence of boundaries (an initial condition in the assignment process) determines empathy patterns in space and so may be influential in keeping the 'optimum' pattern of boundaries (and assignments) in their original configuration.

In the second place, redistribution policy may (partly because of the bonds of empathy just mentioned) call for negotiated direct intergovernmental payments between jurisdictions. These are not the same as the accidental and confusing cross-boundary flows of non-governmental goods and payments which often suggest that political maps have been drawn in spite of, not because of, the ties of trade and factor movements. Rather, they are government payments (or 'grants') by which governments are carrying out domestic demands to augment the incomes of people outside their own borders. They are a means by which people in a small region, unable to obtain widespread consent from people in a wider (ie, more senior) jurisdiction to policies to assist residents in another region, utilize their own regional government to make payments (or subsidies in kind) to recipients living in another jurisdiction at the same level.[13] The fewness of such payments in Canada and the United States suggests that perhaps citizen investment in signalling to a senior government has a higher payoff than in investing in persuading low-level governments to undertake equivalent interjurisdictional transfers.[14]

The third comment concerns the use of both co-ordination and administration activities as 'substitutes' for investment by citizens in migration. By substitutes we refer to governmental activity to moderate (or head off) citizen migration.

To begin the analysis, we consider a strong case in which empathy, if it exists, stretches only to a citizen's own family and near neighbours. People in jurisdiction J have no concern for people outside J. Under these circumstances government redistribution policies, both when they are induced by the 'taking' goals of low-income groups and when they embody the empathy between citizens at all income levels, are threatened by the potential migration of citizens. There are two

13 The citizens desiring to make the payments may be pictured as having two alternatives: signalling to their senior government their demand for an inter-regional redistribution; or signalling to their lower level government their demand for a policy of helping people in another (outside) region. The regional government receiving these signals then has three alternative ways of implementing this demand: using the senior government as a vehicle for inter-regional payments; making direct inter-regional government to government payments; or making transfers directly to selected citizens abroad. The third method requires less co-ordination than the first two.

14 Another hypothesis is that interjurisdictional empathy is negligible. But this hypothesis is not supported by casual observation. Instead, one is aware of demands in Quebec to assist persons of the same language on the prairies and in New Brunswick, Jews in New York and Irish in Massachusetts to help their co-religionists abroad, and similar strong bonds between Ukrainians, Mennonites, Armenians, Tibetans, and other dispersed people. In all these cases one observes non-governmental flows of assistance, facilitated (and sometimes augmented) by the co-ordination activities of top level governments. Municipal, state, and provincial co-ordination activities do exist, but are not depended on.

dangers: rich or unfavoured taxpayers may leave; and poor or favoured recipients may immigrate.[15]

Can the potential exodus of taxpayers be reduced? National governments do appear to have been assigned powers that can prevent immigration, but few lower-level jurisdictions have powers to exercise policy functions or administrative activities that will reduce the rate of departure. A few devices do occur: pensions can be non-portable, property transfers regulated and discouraged, and outward travel made costly. Furthermore, potential immigrants can perhaps be bribed to stay by policies that hold them to enjoy subsidized schools, theatres, or amenities tailored to their tastes, or to work in jobs protected by local patronage.

Anti-emigration co-ordination policies also may be imagined: governments not only can refuse export visas, passports, birth certificates, or foreign exchange where these are essential for moving, but also attempt to persuade other governments not to receive migrants.[16]

But we do not observe much conscious use of either of these official deterrants to migration, at least by lower-level jurisdictions. Instead, measures seem to be used chiefly by jurisdictions of immigration to prevent or reduce the arrival of poor transfer recipients. Both co-ordination activities and administration activities have been employed.

Administrative steps are probably the least costly. Versions of those to be mentioned are to be found in many federations, especially in Switzerland, where intercantonal moving is less easy than in North America. Chief among these are residence requirements: conditions attached to the right to enjoy both transfers and such non-public government services as schooling, health care, or public housing that specify minimum periods of residence, citizenship, or labour-force status. Others are the continued use of such regulations as those dealing with land zoning, foreign ownership of real property, foreign control of indsutry, nationality of language of workers, health or disease immunization, inherited defects, and licensing of professions. These are blunt instruments, however, and we do not find them used effectively in most low-level jurisdictions. The chief reason is probably that it is costly to administer them in such a way as only to deter unwelcome immigration. Used too vigorously, they burden new arrivals who, being rich or in other ways welcome, must nevertheless suffer the same disabilities as

15 Readers of an earlier draft of this chapter have assured us that these two dangers did materialize and overwhelmed New York City's redistribution schemes, eventually causing that city's bankruptcy.
16 There are other steps that governments could try. Variants of extradition, as now used in tax treaties and in criminal law, are possibilities. And the recent campaign against the international brain drain has suggested means by which governments could retrieve some of their former residents. But these are remedies to be used in desperation only.

poor immigrants. In any case, they tend to be abolished because they antagonize both established citizens who are friends of new arrivals, and new citizens who have endured them before achieving local citizenship. Thus, while low-level jurisdictions' restrictions may sometimes protect certain professions and industries against new middle-class arrivals, such administrative activities are likely to be less effective in preventing the immigration of dependents or families with low incomes. This job is handled by interjurisdiction co-ordination.

Consider a low-level jurisdiction that proposes to introduce a generous redistributional system. How can it prevent an influx of the poor? It can use co-ordination activities to head off citizens who would otherwise move in. These activities may lead to either or both of two instruments to reduce a poor citizen's incentive to migrate: agreement on a 'national minimum standard' of transfers or social services; and provision of grants or other payments that will raise the standards of transfers and social services under the government in the jurisdiction from which the migrants come.

Either of these can be direct, involving co-ordination between jurisdictions' governments, or indirect, involving negotiations with and participation by a senior government. In Canada, at least, examples of all possibilities can be observed, except of making payments directly from one province to another.[17] Thus we find national minimum standards of some social services agreed directly between provinces, and others agreed by the provinces with the central government. We also find the rich provinces criticizing the present equalization (non-conditional grant) scheme on the grounds that it makes payments to governments and not to people; we interpret this as support for grants, coupled with regret that the grant scheme does not selectively head off potential immigrants to Ontario, Alberta, and British Columbia. But the government-to-government grant scheme is more likely to win acceptance in the receiving area. Not only does part of the funds find its way to citizens who now need not move to obtain greater benefits, but another part can be regarded as a reduction of actual or potential taxes paid by higher-income groups (also potential migrants). Thus, as compensation for retaining its poorer and more dependent citizens, the government of the jurisdiction is able to retain its richer taxpayers.

It will be obvious that redistribution policies will stimulate co-ordination and

17 This has been proposed as a less complicated way than equalization of transferring oil royalties and other natural resource windfalls from resource rich to other provinces. Something like it is also to be found in Germany. See J.S.H. Hunter, *Revenue Sharing in the Federal Republic of Germany* (Canberra: Centre for Research on Federal Financial Relations, Australian National University 1973). We have also been told by an anonymous referee that the old imperial government of China had a regular system under which some provinces made payments to others.

administration activities which, even if they are formally similar to government organization activities in connection with other functions, appear to play an important role in preventing redistributional policies from being ineffective when they are assigned to lower-level jurisdictions. This role for co-ordination seems not to have been noticed by other writers, who describe a process in which taxpayers and transfer recipients wander, unimpeded, among jurisdictions until some final migratory equilibrium is reached. Co-ordinated restraints on migration are not mentioned.[18]

How will co-ordination (and supporting administrative activities) vary with γ the degree of centralization? It follows from what we have said above that they will respond to citizen mobility. The latter will tend to fall, as γ increases. The result should be as follows: when redistribution is extremely decentralized, citizens will be attracted to migrate short distances to obtain relief from unsatisfactory policies. Governments will respond to this potentially vigorous citizen mobility by high investment in administrative and co-ordinating measures. As γ increases, opportunities for beneficial citizen moving will diminish, while co-ordination will be both less expensive and less necessary. When redistribution has become completely centralized, mobility ceases and with it co-ordination. Citizens will then have recourse only to signalling and governments to administrative activities, as described in Chapter 7.

Assignment
We may now bring together the four components of organization activity. The formal part of our treatment need not be long because little has been discovered in our survey of the four components that does not also apply to some extent to the organization activity surrounding other functions. However, the models of Part Two are in need of modification because of three quantitative differences between investment in organization activities in connection with redistribution and that in connection with other functions: there is likely to be a greater stimulus to citizen mobility; there may be greater use of co-ordination to head off or deter citizen mobility; and there is some possibility that interdependent utilities (empathy) will confuse or even reverse the attitudes and actions outlined in Chapters 7 and 8.

To the extent that the four activities do respond to changes in γ as outlined in Part Two, nothing new need be said here. This similarity between the assignment

18 Buchanan and other authors do mention the possibility of a tax or price on migration. See J.M. Buchanan and C.J. Goetz, 'Efficiency Limits to Fiscal Mobility,' *Journal of Public Economics* II, 1 (April 1972) 25-44; Flatters, Henderson, and Mieszkowski, 'Public Goods, Efficiency, and Regional Fiscal Equalization'; and J.M. Buchanan, 'Who Should Distribute What in a Federal System?' in H.M. Hochman and G.E. Peterson, eds, *Redistribution through Public Choice* (New York: Columbia University Press 1974) 34.

of redistribution and other functions would be greatest if citizen mobility were costly and empathy strong but geographically localized. There would be no overriding reason to predict that redistribution should be a centralized, or national, function: all or parts of it might be found distributed at all levels. This conclusion is, we believe, confirmed by observation that in international affairs, different redistribution policies can successfully be carried out by small, Balkanized nation states. Because empathy between citizens is often low, and mobility discouraged, each state, no matter how small it (or its budget) is, can pursue its own redistributive goals.

When we relax the assumption about mobility, however, we come to the conditions that are most often assumed in the literature on federal finance. With citizen empathy lacking and mobility easy, redistribution at the local level cannot be pursued independently. Each local government must match what is done elsewhere by explicitly concerting its policy with that of other jurisdictions, or allowing a senior government implicitly or explicitly to assume the lion's share of the job. Such reactions have been correctly looked on as informal acts of reassignment, confirming that redistribution cannot be assigned to small local jurisdictions.

As we have pointed out in the previous subsection, however, this conclusion does neglect some potentialities of government co-ordination and administrative activities. The explicit matching of policies or handing over of functions are already types of co-ordination. We feel that the use of other types of co-ordination should also be acknowledged. Prominent among these is the widespread support given to the principle of minimum standards, or uniformity, by provincial governments. While this support could be explained by strong feelings of cross-continental empathy, we would argue that it should also be explained by attempts to reduce, or head off, citizen mobility. Other provincial bargaining attitudes, as well as policies, also reveal the use of co-ordination and administration to reduce mobility. Among these are provincial consent to or even encouragement of equalization and tax-sharing schemes; provincial regard for 'national solidarity' in interprovincial bargaining about prices of resources and energy; and agreement that one and only one bargain must be struck with all provinces by the national government in shared-cost health and education schemes.

Furthermore, we are impressed by the prevalence of administrative deterrents to citizen mobility.[19] Residence requirements for eligibility for social services are most prominent among these, but the reader should also consult the list given in the previous subsection for others.

19 See Albert Breton, *Discriminating Government Policies in Federal Countries* (Montreal: C.D. Howe Institute 1967).

The existence of these co-ordination and administrative activities provides indirect evidence of an operational decentralization of redistribution to the provincial level. The provinces are already carrying out their own redistribution policies, and these differ between provinces. The interprovincial differences stimulate potential migration among the provinces. This is neutralized or kept in check by the governments' investments in co-ordination and administrative activities.

Finally, when we introduce not only mobility but also the possibility of important citizen empathy for citizens in other provinces, we find that previous generalizations about the working of decentralized redistribution simply are not specific or robust enough to lead to any conclusions. To see this, the reader has only to consider the vast number of possible types of behaviour open to citizens who wish to help others. For example, one possibility is that citizens with empathy for others may individually move and vote in such a way as to increase the satisfaction they get from the improvement in the circumstances of others. Obviously, costs of voting and of moving will constrain this behaviour. But, unconstrained, it may lead to the rich moving *towards* areas of low incomes and expensive redistributive systems; and the poor moving away from regions where transfers place a heavy burden on the rich.

Alternatively, all citizens may have empathy for others, but may choose to act as free riders. In this case the rich will flee from the poor, if the redistribution is decentralized. It is not clear how the poor will behave, without other assumptions about desire to be near or remote.

In these differing circumstances, co-ordination and administrative activities might sometimes be used to discourage, but at other times to encourage, mobility. Governments may even, on behalf of their citizens, facilitate a gathering in of transfer recipients, and it is possible that, if empathy is a function of geographical distance, total redistribution would be greater under extremely low values of γ than under extreme centralization.

Let us apply these ideas. We would guess that, while in the real world of Canadian and American federalism, partial redistribution is not an overwhelmingly attractive or repellent aspect of government platforms, mobility between provinces and states certainly is an ever present citizen opportunity. Empathy between provinces certainly exists, and the possibilities of co-ordination are still being explored and tried out. Assuming these conditions, what assignment of partial redistribution should be predicted? The strongest conclusion we can come to is a negative one: partial redistribution need not be highly centralized. Much 'taking' or zero-sum redistribution that arouses strong opposition will be assigned to the national government. This is a conclusion explicitly reached by Buchanan. But empathy also exists and suggests the desirability of joint occupation of redistributive functions.

When empathy is strong, partial redistribution is implemented because people like R have empathy for other citizens, both in their own and in other jurisdictions. That the strength of these bonds may weaken with distance may require a complex system of redistribution. Some citizens may depend on high-level governments, with their greater geographical span and larger population, to make transfers on a non-selective basis to citizens abroad and to citizens in other jurisdictions.[20] In addition, citizens like R may wish to make larger, and more selective, transfers to citizens closer to them. These might be governed by a residence requirement. Thus the minimization of all organizational costs as they relate to redistribution could, and apparently does, lead to concurrent authority in this area.

Put formally, the tentative conclusions above stem from a very simple characteristic of organization activities: as γ increases, one type of organization activity is replaced by another. That is, they are substitutes. This means that, to the extent that the constituent assembly is seeking that degree of centralization at which the total cost of investment in organization activities is minimized, γ^* will have no *automatic* tendency to move at once towards $\gamma^* = 0$ or $\gamma^* = 1$. Intermediate values are quite possible when only one redistributive instrument is to be assigned; and joint occupation of the redistributive field when the assignment of several instruments of partial redistribution is in question.

3 GENERAL REDISTRIBUTION

In this section we discuss the assignment of the power or responsibility to alter the *general* distribution of incomes. The definitions and assumptions which allow us to distinguish this function from partial redistribution were presented in Section 1. In brief, our intention in this section is to inquire into the assignment of the power to maintain or to alter the over-all balance of power, wealth, and consumption among regions, age cohorts, social classes, and income groups.

In many ways, everything said in the previous section applies equally well to the assignment of general redistribution. A nation of small jurisdictions, each of which was prone to undertake large-scale and disturbing changes in over-all income distribution, would be subject to the same organization activities by citizens and governments as a similar nation prone only to modest changes in its use of instruments of redistribution (such as old age pensions). Migration and the threat of migration would play an important part in motivating citizen response to redis-

20 These would be the recipients about whom each government's foreign aid and poverty program bureaus report to their respective citizenry. For example, Canadians receive reports from CIDA about overseas needs, and from Statistics Canada and from various administrative departments about income redistributions within Canada.

tributive proposals; and the need for co-ordination between governments would also be significant. We would guess that the potential influence of migration would be more influential than in the assignment of partial redistribution powers, and would further speculate that this might produce a larger degree of centralization. That is our model, applied to general redistribution, might suggest that this function should be left to central governments rather than to local bodies.

Consideration of this conclusion, however, raises some doubts about the applicability of the model. In simple language, it seems to be saying that, because general redistribution implies large changes, even regarded by the substantial minority perhaps as confiscations, the constituent assembly will make sure that those who disagree cannot move away, but must submit. To prevent their moving away, a high degree of centralization would be needed. But our model's concept of the constituent assembly does not have this policy purpose in view; and we therefore discuss in this section the suitability of the organization-cost approach for predicting the assignment of policies leading to massive, non-incremental, social changes.

With a given initial distribution of income among three groups, each group will employ political action in order to move the general distribution of income towards their respective ideals. Whether the decision of any group prevails depends on its relative size, for each faces a coalition of the other two that would block such a redistribution.

The outcome is indeterminate if the groups are of equal size. It is true that Pareto-optimal analysis shows that in a choice between a position between extreme inequality and distributions intermediate between the ideal distributions of the three groups, the latter will be preferred by all. But if the choice is not limited to such a pair, coalitions of two groups may well prefer less egalitarian outcomes. (And the stability of these coalitions will be vulnerable to offers from the excluded group.)

In general, however, we are distrustful of voting analyses of general redistribution within a particular jurisdiction, unless there has been a marked change of preferences by a large proportion of the electorate. We sympathize with those who argue that the underlying constitution, in which the voting rules are contained, is likely to be based, implicitly, on the absence of large-scale redistributions. Peaceful general redistribution would seem inconsistent with constant preferences, and consistent only with a more profound change in social attitudes. Such a profound change is likely to involve, *inter alia*, the reassignment of many functions; it is not likely that the structure of government will be maintained. Consequently, there may be no point in a precautionary assignment of responsibility for general redistribution; until demand for it comes, it must remain unassigned.

A more extreme way of stating this is to identify partial redistribution with marginal changes, and general redistribution with total – indeed revolutionary – changes. To whom should total reform, revolutionary redistribution, be assigned in the structure of government? Signalling and mobility will indeed vary with the size of jurisdiction across which the redistribution is to take place, but a nice calculation of their costs may seem too unimportant to influence the constituent assembly's choice of assignment. 'Legitimacy' and 'sovereignty' are threatened by revolutionary redistributions that spread too far, and 'natural rights' are invoked by regions from which redistributions are denied.

What is involved here by the invocation of such slogans is suggested in Section 2 that while citizens are interested in redistributive policies, they may be assumed not to have preferences concerning who was to administer them. Is this assumption sustainable in this section? When extreme – or revolutionary – changes in the general distribution of income are at issue, citizens will strive to express not only the intensity, but also the geographical span of their empathy, jealousy, and indifference. These will be revealed as citizen preferences for assignment of the general redistributive functions, and will become direct inputs into the activities of the constituent assembly.

In particular, they will infect the proceedings of constituent assemblies of the representative government type, discussed in Chapter 8. Politicians and bureaucrats may be identified with partisan positions in the redistributive struggle. Assignment becomes then merely one aspect of larger issues. Our model is ambitious, but we are not so immodest as to suggest that it can predict the assignment of redistribution under such circumstances.

11

Special problems in
the assignment of stabilization functions

I INTRODUCTION

In this chapter we discuss the forces that impinge on the assignment of the stabilization functions in a federal structure. The special problems that pertain to stabilization are not difficulties in applying the approach outlined in Part Two, but in understanding how and in what direction a change in the centralization of stabilization powers can cause a change in organizational activities and in organizational costs. Once such relationships have been mapped out, the comparative statics of the assignment process are fairly straightforward.

The stabilization functions were defined in Chapter 2. Involving the smoothing out, at a desired level, of fluctuations in such aggregates as total output, employment, and the level of prices, they are defined in terms of intentions rather than in terms of the stabilization instruments used. In the absence of stabilization policies, such fluctuations may induce citizens to invest in mobility or signalling when they are concerned about inflation, unemployment, or both. The question addressed in this chapter is how the assignment of stabilization functions to alternative jurisdictional levels can affect the total amount of mobility and signalling by citizens and of administration and co-ordination activities by governments.

Since our intent is only to illustrate these matters we have greatly simplified and formalized typical conjunctural situations requiring stabilization. The chapter deals with an economy that is vulnerable either to excessive or to deficient aggregate demand. While we shall also mention situations in which domestic prices change because of changes in import prices, we shall not call these changes 'inflationary.' We also rule out inflation stemming from historically justified expectations of rising prices. We are therefore not concerned with the dynamics of business cycles, but simply with their comparative statics, that is, with displacements in the neighbourhood of equilibrium. We also ignore policies appropriate to periods with both rising prices and unemployment.

The outline of the chapter is as follows. In Section 2 we deal with the assignment of 'microeconomic' government powers. The example chosen to illustrate the nature of the problem is the power to become a currency area with a flexible exchange rate. In Section 3 we analyse the assignment of the 'macroeconomic' stabilization powers, focusing (in the first subsection) on fiscal powers alone and (in the second subsection) on the integration of fiscal, monetary, and exchange rate policies, along with such related instruments as the power to intervene in bond and currency markets.

2 MICROECONOMIC STABILIZATION POLICIES

While we recognize that the micro-macro terminology has been applied more often to types of theory than to types of policy, we adopt it here to distinguish between two kinds of government stabilization activity. We shall designate as microeconomic those stabilization policies which do not require that governments recognize the macro effect of their own spending, taxing, and financing. Macroeconomic policies, on the other hand, imply governmental recognition of the macro effects of their own decisions.

Government can in turn provide two types of microeconomic policy. Neither attempts to correct instability directly, but both can mitigate its effects. The first type involves redistribution and the second insulation.

Redistribution – either among people or over time – is a frequent response. Instability manifests itself differentially: the unemployment of the recession and recovery phases of the business cycle is concentrated in certain industries and occupations, while the inflation of the peak period hits other groups. To meet these unintended redistributions, such policies as income transfers (welfare and pension supplements), indexation of financial instruments and of labour contracts, price supports, and wage and price controls have been employed. In addition, governments in such circumstances may manage their net external debt and their aggregate budgets, so as to redistribute disposable income and the supply of public goods between time periods.[1] Neither the motivation for, nor the implementation of, such redistributive policies is sufficiently different from those discussed in our chapters on the assignment of redistribution functions to justify further discussion here.

The second type of microeconomic policy consists of attempts to *insulate* a jurisdiction from fluctuations originating elsewhere. One way of doing this is to

1 For example, various Canadian provinces, in the depression of the 1930s, borrowed to finance current expenditures, hoping to effect repayment when incomes rose again (in the then independent Newfoundland), or when the drought ended (Saskatchewan). More recently, OPEC members are lending their oil profits, just as Alberta did twenty years ago.

reduce market interdependence by means of restrictions on trade, flows of people or capital, or on all of these. A more familiar insulating technique that avoids such direct controls, aims instead at attaining rapid domestic adjustments to fluctuations by promoting price flexibility, either internal or external. Of all such techniques we here deal only with external price stability – that is, with the decision to rely on a flexible exchange rate. Accordingly, it is assumed that nominal factor prices are inflexible downwards.[2]

The question to be discussed is therefore the assignment of the power to insulate the domestic economy by means of a flexible rate. We shall approach the matter by examining the determination of the *size* of the responsible jurisdiction. We follow this approach because size and level are closely associated. If the assignment procedure leads to the conclusion that the power to adopt a flexible exchange rate is to be assigned to a small jurisdictional unit, it is implied also that it should be assigned to a low-level government. Contrariwise, if it is to be assigned to a larger-size jurisdiction, it is implied also that it should be assigned to a higher, national (or even international) government.

Accordingly, we now investigate the effects of the size of a currency area on citizen and government investment in organizational activities. The possibility of basing a positive monetary policy of the power with respect to currency is not discussed until the next section. Here our analysis is reduced to its essentials by comparing organizational activities in 'large' and 'small' regions having their own currencies. Our argument is that the larger the currency area, the more numerous will be the citizens who will be forced to make costly adjustments to an external shock that directly affects the trade of only one region, or 'district.'

This proposition is similar to one common in the balance of payments literature. Imagine a proposed currency union of member districts. We begin by assuming that factors of production are not mobile between districts (each has its own fixed endowment of labour and capital). Whether a particular district should join the union would depend on whether the possible future changes in the common external exchange rate would be appropriate to the expected fluctuations in its own trade. The net advantages of joining depend on the impact of its 'internal' trade with other members of the union, and on its 'external' trade with the rest of the world of having its exchange rate determined by the combined external trade of all districts in the union.

'Internal' effects are those stemming from a district's trade with other parts of a currency union. Under the union, fluctuations in trade with other districts will

2 To be more specific, we assume that nominal wages move upward when the excess demand for labour increases, but do not move down when it decreases. Furthermore, we assume that there is no world- or economy-wide wage setting or bargaining.

not be softened by an exchange rate adjustment. Instead there will be changes in output and employment, leading either to localized unemployment or shortages. While these effects of an inflexible rate may, according to circumstances, be deemed an over-all advantage or disadvantage for the whole district, what is important here are its differing effects on different parts of the district. These will, in the short run, create an incentive to signal.[3]

The 'external' effect may stem from instability in the trade between a district within the union and the world outside. For example, the district's outside trade may go into net deficit, perhaps because of a decline in outside demand, or because an industry, localized in the district, is no longer competitive abroad. Whatever the reason, the union's currency would now depreciate. The extent of the depreciation would depend on the size of the district's declining trade relative to the trade of the whole union.

The smaller the district relative to the entire union, the less effective the depreciation of the union's currency in restoring the district's trade, that is, the smaller the district relative to the union, the more it will be deprived of external price flexibility as a means of adjustment and the more it will suffer unemployment. In the long run, it will experience a greater structural shift away from the declining industry than if its currency could depreciate further.

It follows that the larger the relative size of the district's trade the greater the union's currency depreciation. While a large depreciation will be more appropriate than a small depreciation for the original district's deficit, it will be less welcome among the other districts of the union. The greater the decline in the union exchange rate, the greater the rise in these other districts' price levels owing not only to a rising domestic price of imported goods, but also to an increasing excess demand for their net exports. This tendency will persist until they have adjusted the structure of their industry away from untraded goods to exports and import substitutes.[4]

The effects of a district joining an international currency union are similar to those that would result from the centralization of the power to have separate exchange rates in a federation. The citizens of the new member district of a currency

3 If, contrary to the assumption in the text, labour is mobile, citizens could invest in moving as well as in signalling. And if capital is mobile in the short run, a district's own exchange rate may fluctuate with variations in capital movements, unrelated to trade deficits. Then the 'internal' effects of joining a currency union will include the moderating of such fluctuations, depending on the source or destination of the capital flow.

4 We need not detail the contrary case. One district's increased net exports to the outside world would cause an appreciation of the union currency. The larger the relative size of this district, the greater the appreciation; and so the greater the unemployment and subsequent adjustment imposed on the rest of the union.

union like those of a province in a federation in which the currency power has been reassigned upwards will be exposed to both adverse and favourable internal demand changes in other parts of the union or federation, without the insulation that would be provided by a flexible exchange rate. (Such demand changes are exemplified by the manifestation of unequal regional levels of business activity within one national currency area.)

By adapting the traditional balance of payments literature, which focuses mainly on the conditions for separate currency areas, we examine what happens to these conditions when the size of a small area is expanded. Specifically, we wish to show that as the number of districts in a currency area increases the number of people who are dissatisfied with the value of the common currency (the exchange rate) increases.

To do this, we assume a spatial plain over which workers (citizens) can move. We further assume that this interdistrict mobility is a function of travel costs which vary only with distance.

Now we suppose that a loss of sales by one district of a larger currency area produces a devaluation of the common currency. This devaluation would tend to increase the demand for workers in all traded good industries in all districts of the union, regardless of their distance from the district originally losing sales. It would tend to ease the absorption of workers both in that district and in nearby districts. But it would be of no use, or of negative value, to workers and employers living further away, if they were already fully employed at the previous exchange rate. Thus, when cost of mobility is correlated with distance, a continuous hypothetical increase in the geographical size of the union will reveal a continuous increase in the number of people who are adversely affected by a revaluation.

The smaller the degree of mobility the greater the number of citizens who suffer rising local prices, shortages, or unemployment;[5] and, consequently, the smaller the number of districts that will benefit from being assembled as one currency jurisdiction.

The careful reader will have noted that the labour mobility analysed in the preceding pages must, in the real world, be indistinguishable from the citizen mobility discussed in the model of the structure of the public sector of Part Two. The point that needs to be emphasized, however, is that whereas traditional balance of payment theory considers only labour mobility as an adjustment mechanism, our model of federalism, as applied in the foregoing discussion, raises the

5 Districts may not differ in factor endowments (or comparative advantage in particular products). Industries will then be intermixed. Citizens of one district will work in industries that will both be benefited and harmed by a devaluation. Mobility may be easy. Only gradual regional differentiation can justify not placing all such districts in the same currency area.

additional possibility that by changing the degree of centralization, that is, by re-assigning the currency power downwards, the constituent assembly can reduce the extent of disequilibrium or frustration and therefore the need for mobility.

We should recall that in the assignment model citizens are not confined to mobility as a response to disequilibrium; they may also engage in signalling. Furthermore, the extent to which they move or signal will depend on the amount that governments invest in co-ordination and administration. It is not impossible that when exchange rates are flexible the need for co-ordination and administration may be very limited – this is a merit that is often claimed for flexible rates. In such a case the assignment of the currency power might be governed exclusively by mobility and signalling activities.

So far we have not considered two additional consequences of having flexible exchange rates: transactions costs and uncertainty. The more currencies there are, the more exchange rate calculations must be undertaken, and the higher the cost of transacting. In addition, fluctuating exchange rates give rise to uncertainty, and if citizens are averse to risk this uncertainty will lead to the loss of profits from forgone deals; to the costs of hedging and engaging in forward markets; and to the cost of obtaining information about currency values and trends.

Because of these transaction costs and uncertainty citizens will be induced to invest in signalling and mobility the amounts of which we would expect to increase with the decentralization of this function. For the same reasons, governments may be induced to invest in administration and co-ordination activities.[6]

3 MACROECONOMIC STABILIZATION POLICIES

We turn now to the power to implement macroeconomic stabilization policies. How do the effects on citizens of the assignment of the responsibility both for monetary, fiscal, and debt management policies vary with the level and size of jurisdictions? To examine this we adapt the approach of the previous section: we examine the impact on citizens of hypothetically enlarging the area of a jurisdiction within which a single macroeconomic policy is conducted. Enlarging a policy area is again assumed to be equivalent to assigning the function to a higher jurisdictional level.

In the course of our examination we recognize two new elements that were neglected in the previous section. First, macroeconomic policies involve leakages

6 For example, investment in mobility may take place, if it is possible for traders, by moving to reduce the burden of transactions costs. Similarly, investment in co-ordination may be undertaken if, by agreements between jurisdictions, traders can be assisted to deal in recognized key currencies, or if by forming a currency union it is possible for autonomous jurisdictions to agree on a single currency.

into other regions. Thus the benefits of these policies will be experienced in part by citizens outside the originating jurisdiction. Secondly, macroeconomic policies involve a change in the burden of taxes on the citizens of a region. Thus in a jurisdiction of a given size, macroeconomic policies will confer benefits that need not be enjoyed by the same citizens who bear their burden. Furthermore, if the area of the jurisdiction is changed, the balance between those who gain and those who lose will change.

To simplify the discussion we will divide the analysis into two subsections. In the first, it will be assumed that jurisdictions can conduct fiscal but not monetary policy. That is, they must operate either by changing the size of their total budget (both spending and taxing), or by borrowing or retiring debt.

But fiscal policy can rarely be used alone because the consequent debt operations have an effect both on financial markets serving the private sector of the same jurisdiction and on the external value of the currency. To handle this question, we turn in the second subsection to the assignment of the power over monetary policy, as a complement to fiscal policy. This assignment in turn is dependent on whether or not the jurisdiction has its own currency or is part of a larger currency area, and so is closely linked to the problem of currency areas already analysed in Section 2.

Fiscal policy only
In this subsection we consider the effects of varying the size of the jurisdiction responsible for fiscal policy. We assume that the supply of money is given. It follows that the government must have recourse to money markets whenever its fiscal operations result in a change in its debt position.

To proceed with our investigation, we consider first of all a fiscal policy that has a definite and recognizable initial burden: the policy of dealing with inflation by increasing personal income taxes. To simplify we assume factor supplies to be given and that the effect of the tax increase is to reduce private consumption spending, consequently preventing the price increase that would otherwise take place.

Whether those who pay the increased tax will experience the benefit[7] depends upon the extent of the market within which excess demand is experienced. The taxpaying group might be smaller, or larger than, this market. At one extreme, most prices in one jurisdiction of taxpayers may be substantially determined by outside demand. Then taxation would have a significant effect only on the prices of non-traded – wholly domestic – goods. At the other extreme, interregional

7 Since government expenditures are assumed constant, the term 'benefit' refers unequivocally to the price effect of the tax increase.

trade might be conducted at prices determined within the taxing jurisdiction. Then the local tax policy would affect both local prices and those outside. In both cases, the effects of tax policy would spill, in or out, across jurisdictional lines. Only with no interjurisdictional trade could there be an exact correspondence between the political area levying the tax and the market area within which fiscal policy would affect prices.

This, to begin our examination of the effects of hypothetically expanding a fiscal policy region, the initial impact of increased taxation, applied in an extremely small jurisdiction, will spill into and be dissipated among the neighbouring small jurisdictions. Consolidating all such jurisdictions will increase the number of non-traded goods in each jurisdiction as well as reduce the number of traded goods, the prices of which are determined elsewhere. That is, consolidating fiscal policy regions will reduce the number of citizens whose real incomes are influenced by prices determined outside the jurisdiction, and consequently will reduce the number of citizens who either bear a net tax burden or reap a net tax benefit.

Those citizens who bear a net tax burden possibly will seek to reduce that burden through signalling or mobility. Signalling would be chosen by those citizens who expected that the government could change the pattern of taxation in their favour. Mobility would be chosen by those who estimated the yield on such signalling to be too low. However, citizens would choose neither signalling nor mobility if the yield on co-ordination were high. That yield would be high if the taxing government could induce governments of neighbouring jurisdictions also to engage in the same fiscal policy. One would expect that when the number of jurisdictions is very large, co-ordination costs would be so high as to deter attempts at fiscal policy co-ordination. In view of the fact that changes in the size of jurisdictions correspond to changes in the degree of centralization, it follows that by reassigning the fiscal policy function the constituent assembly can influence the amount of resources invested in organizational activity.

If we switch from fiscal policy aimed at inflation to one aimed at unemployment the analysis is very similar. Assume that a jurisdiction is part of a larger currency area and capital market. If expansionary fiscal policy requires a deficit, it will be financed by an increase in debt. The service of this debt must be financed by future taxation. Such taxation will have a 'burden' similar to that discussed above in connection with a tax policy directed at inflation. Consequently, there is no important difference between the analysis of the two cases.

So far we have implicitly assumed that citizens and governments had no preferences concerning the redistributional aspects of fiscal policy. If, however, it is recognized that such preferences exist, and that they differ not only between citizens, but also between concentrations of citizens in different jurisdictions, it follows that reassigning fiscal policy powers upwards will induce citizens and governments to invest more heavily in organizational activities. Why? Simply because such a reassignment must involve either a uniform fiscal policy over all jurisdictions or one which discriminates among preferences. The first case implies large investments in signalling activities; the second large investments in administration (mostly in search) activities.[8]

To summarize, in this subsection we have dealt with the variation in organizational costs that result from changes in the centralization of fiscal policy powers. We have also seen that both investment in signalling and in administration, especially in search, will increase with centralization. This last conclusion is important, since it suggests that the assignment of the fiscal policy functions to larger jurisdictions may lead to higher total organizational costs than its assignment to smaller – and more numerous – jurisdictions. This runs counter to the orthodox generalization which asserts that 'higher is better' when the level of fiscal policy responsibility is discussed.

Both conclusions, however, have been reached by abstracting from the assignment of powers with respect to monetary policy, that is, by assuming that all jurisdictional levels and all jurisdictions at each level would use the same currency and that capital mobility was such that all could borrow and lend in the same capital market. In the next section we abandon this assumption and analyse how fiscal and monetary policy functions are assigned.

Monetary and fiscal policies together
In this subsection, we discuss the assignment of powers with respect to both fiscal and monetary policy. Whereas in the previous subsection, variations in the supply of money were taken as given, that is were assumed not to be an instrument of stabilization policy, in this subsection that instrument is assumed to be used by governments at whatever jurisdictional level it is assigned.

The first matter that must be cleared up is that of the meaning that attaches to the implications of assigning the power with respect to monetary policy. That power must include among other things responsibility for the domestic and foreign value of a currency. When the power with respect to monetary policy is assigned to a particular jurisdictional level, it must be understood that each of the jurisdictions at that level carries the responsibility for the value of its own particular currency. For example, if the monetary policy power in Canada was assigned to the provincial level, that assignment would imply the existence of ten provincial currencies, of ten provincial central banks or equivalent institutions, and of

---

8 If centralization is complete, investment in mobility and co-ordination must necessarily be zero. However, if centralization is incomplete – the power is reassigned to (say) the provincial level – investment in these two activities will take place, in addition to those mentioned in the text.

exchange rates between all these currencies and between each of them and the other currencies in the world.

There is nothing in the definitions of the previous paragraph that rules out the assignment of this power to more than one jurisdictional level. Although there are interesting problems that could be worked out for the case of concurrent authority with respect to monetary policy, fiscal policy, or both, nothing additional concerning the assignment problem would be learnt from a discussion of these cases. Consequently, we do not return to these possibilities.

Before proceeding we must consider the evantuality of competitive devaluation of currencies when the monetary policy power is assigned to any jurisdictional level below the national one. This follows from the fact that each jurisdiction can hope to gain by aggressive beggar-thy-neighbour policies. It is hard to deny that such a phenomenon will have an impact on the assignment of monetary policy power. That impact, however, cannot be understood without reference to organizational activities, particularly co-ordination. Low co-ordination costs can lead to agreement among the jurisdictions to avoid competitive devaluations. High co-ordination costs on the other hand may lead to the elimination of such devaluations by an upward reassignment of the power.

We now turn to the problem of the assignment of the monetary and fiscal policy powers. In general, irrespective of the jurisdictional level to which the fiscal policy power has been assigned, it is possible to envisage that the monetary policy power can be assigned to the same, to a higher, or to a lower level, and conversely. We must emphasize that there is nothing technically infeasible about dividing responsibility for macroeconomic policy between two levels of jurisdictions. For example, a central government can conduct fiscal policy, while provincial governments are responsible for monetary matters. A national fiscal deficit could be financed by having the central government placing its bonds with all or some provincial central banks. Alternatively, with a different assignment, provincial fiscal authorities could use the national central bank to finance their deficits. The exact assignment outcome will depend on the cost configuration of the various organizational activities.

We need not discuss the four components of organizational activities as they apply to the assignment of the two stabilization powers. The forces that lead citizens and governments to engage in them are not different from those described in Part Two, and earlier sections of this chapter.

In concluding, it is interesting to note that when governments do not engage in co-ordination activities there will be a convergence of powers over fiscal and monetary policies at the same jurisdictional level. The reason for this is that in the absence of co-ordination between the two levels, the senior government, seeking to generate a fiscal deficit, would have no control over the amount of its debt that it could monetize. The various lower-level central banks would monetize as much or as little as they chose. The lower-level central banks would tend to keep pace with each other, mindful of the effect on their local exchange rates of different changes in money supplies and interest rates. Thus the system of lower-level central banks will expand or contract as though it was controlled by the senior level – as though the powers had been assigned to the same level.

Conversely, if the senior level of government is responsible for monetary policy and the junior level for fiscal policy, the results just derived apply *mutatis mutandis*. If the monetary authorities refuse to monetize provincial debt, they are essentially conducting fiscal policy, while if they automatically monetize this debt, the junior governments are effectively conducting monetary policy. Thus again the two powers will have been assigned to the same level.

4 CONCLUSION

In this chapter we have attempted to establish three propositions. First, we have attempted to show that stabilization policy need not be conducted by 'national' governments. Both micro and macro stabilization policies can be carried out at various levels. Second, we have shown that organizational costs will vary with the level chosen. Third, we have shown that while it is feasible to assign powers pertaining to a different level than the currency and monetary policy powers are assigned, co-ordination problems might tend to place the assignment of powers to implement macroeconomic stabilization policies at one of the two levels only. But, to reiterate, that level need not be the 'national' level.

12

The role of grants in
the assignment process

1 INTRODUCTION

We have, in the preceding chapters, proposed two models of constituent assembly behaviour and examined how the structure of the public sector would be determined and changed when certain parameters were altered. But, except for a few brief comments and digressions, we treated the various classes of functions – regulatory, supply, revenue, redistribution, and stabilization – as if they were independent of each other.

Essentially, we proceeded as if decisions about the assignment of functions and hence about the structure of the public sector could be made with respect to each class of power or function one by one. In the cost minimization model, for example, we suggested that the regulatory and supply functions would be assigned in such a way as to minimize the amount of resources allocated to signalling, mobility, administration, and co-ordination. We implied that revenue functions might be assigned in the same way, without prior assignment of the regulatory and supply functions and assumed a similar independence for other classes of functions.

We did indicate (in Chapter 7, Section 2) that this process could lead to the assignment of some regulatory and supply functions – a class that jointly we may call allocation functions – to jurisdictional levels to which the assigned revenue powers or tax bases might not permit the collection of a sufficiently large revenue to meet the demands of citizens for policies under these allocation functions. In such circumstances, we pointed out that it might not be possible, in the absence of further arrangements, for the governments at the jurisdictional levels that had been assigned these allocation functions to provide the policies citizens expected of them. We indicated that one could interpret the role of grants in federal decentralized structures to be that of improving the matching of assigned revenue and allocation functions.

In this chapter, we would like to extend this view of co-ordinating payments and in particular to examine how, in general, the problem of divergent spans between the revenue and the other functions will be resolved. Pointing out that a revenue-expenditure imbalance is just one of a wider set of possible divergences between the spans of differing functions (or policies under those functions), we suggest that many other types of payment among governments are, in fact, similar in origin. All such can be regarded as contractual payments between jurisdictional levels, between adjoining jurisdictions, or both. This is the subject of the next two sections.

There is a second class of interjurisdictional payments, to which we turn in Section 4. There we take up a prediction in our representative government model of assignment which could not, except by coincidence, arise from the working of a least-cost model. The adjustments in the former model, we argued, could lead the governing politicians of a jurisdictional level that is well endowed with revenue sources, to 'buy' functions or powers from less well-endowed politicians at another level. The permanent (or temporary) financial flows having their origin in such transactions will reveal themselves as a second type of grant.

Finally, in Section 5, we take account of the fact that grants may also be a means of implementing the demands of citizens for economic stabilization, interregional redistribution, or both.

2 GRANTS AS CONTRACTUAL DISBURSEMENTS OF TAX REVENUES

In this section we discuss those interjurisdictional payments that arise from the exploitation of economies of scale in tax collection.

To begin, let us consider an initial, arbitrarily given, assignment table. Let us suppose that this table is such that governments at all levels can, if they so desire, balance their budgets. To put it differently, imagine that all governments at all jurisdictional levels have been assigned revenue and expenditure functions – the term we may use here to cover the total of supply, regulatory, redistribution, and stabilization functions – in such a way that they can find tax rates to yield the revenue to finance whatever expenditure policies they choose.

Would such an assignment table necessarily assure the minimization of the cost of organizational activities? Alternatively, would it necessarily commend itself to the *constituants* of the representative government model? The answer to both these questions is negative: that every government should be self-sufficient in taxes it collects itself is not a necessary condition for the choice of an assignment table.

To demonstrate this proposition, we examine it first in the cost-minimization model and then in the representative government model. Consider then the situation that arises when the existence of economies of scale suggests that tax collection be concentrated or centralized under the administration of one or very few governments. Such will require a negotiated agreement between governments that one of them collect the taxes, coupled with a series of understanding about the permissible changes in the rate structure, in the allowable deductions and exemptions, the timing and manner of disbursement of the proceeds among the consenting members, and possibly the auditing or policing mechanism. These agreements and understandings are, in terms of investment in organizational activities, costly to reach and maintain. Suppose, however, that the general level of co-ordination costs was low enough to justify exploiting the assumed economies of scale in tax collection. We would then see one junior government, say a provincial or municipal one, collecting taxes and disbursing the proceeds to the other junior governments.

We do not observe many actual arrangements of this kind.[1] Apparently the saving of internal administration costs implied by the existence of economies of scale in tax collection is more than offset by other costs, not only those incurred by citizens, but also those incurred by the governments who have delegated tax collection. Consider what may be involved. Each government may accept that its own taxation laws and practices be enforced against its own citizens by another government[2] or, to mitigate the unpopularity of such a mechanism, it may co-operate in setting up a joint tax-collecting service, belonging to no particular jurisdiction, but acting for them all[3] or it may accept the loss of independence inherent in making its tax laws and practices uniform with those of other jurisdictions.

What we do observe is centralized tax collection. This is surely because the alternatives just mentioned are unacceptable, and consequently the outcome of cost-minimization calculations is to assign those tax bases exhibiting economies of scale in collection to a higher level of government. This can be regarded as a substitute for farming out tax collection to a selected junior government. Natur-

1 But they do exist or have existed. For example, a possible arrangement for a customs union is that the 'border' states collect tariffs and perhaps excises for the 'interior' states. In Canada, the Union (1841–67) had an arrangement by which Lower Canadian ports remitted tariff revenues to Upper Canada.

2 In his assessment of French tax farming, Adam Smith surveys some of the advantages and disadvantages of separating the tax collector from the surveillance of the government that passes the tax laws. He is equivocal on whether the lack of 'bowels of compassion' in the tax farmer is, on balance, a disadvantage of the system. In a short sentence or two he mentions one advantage to the government: when revenue from a tax base is uncertain, the uncertainty was borne by the farmer, who paid a certain rent to the sovereign (*The Wealth of Nations*, New York: Modern Library 1937; original 1776, Book V, Chapter 2).

3 A structure of that kind currently exists in the Federal Republic of West Germany.

ally, the exact legal form and outward manifestation of the relations among the junior governments and between them and the senior government will differ greatly from what would be apparent if tax collection had remained at the lower level. But the payments observable in the former system can most profitably be regarded and analysed as if they were not 'grants' bestowed as a favour or indulgence on junior jurisdictions, but deliveries of sums of tax revenue, net of collection expenses, called for by prior negotiations and agreements between payers and payees.

Thus our answer to the question posed about the necessity of a budget-balancing assignment table can be stated as follows: in assigning revenue and expenditure functions, a cost-minimizing constituent assembly will disregard the fact that some jurisdictions may not have the tax bases needed and hence the revenue required to implement the expenditure policies under the powers assigned to them, if it can satisfy itself that the co-ordination activities of governments will permit, at low cost, the payment of money by those to whom tax bases have been assigned without corresponding expenditure functions to those in the opposite circumstance. To state our argument in another way, the 'mismatching' of expenditure and revenue functions – implying that some jurisdictions have the possibility of raising less revenue than is required by their desired level of expenditures (essentially because the yield of tax bases varies), while others can raise more – could, and in general will, be observed in cost-minimizing equilibrium if the yield on investment in co-ordination activities is such as to allow the various jurisdictions to exploit the economies of scale that may exist in tax collection.

The extent of mismatching, and the amount of the consequent interjurisdictional payments, will depend on the size of the economies of scale, the rate of interest, and the costs of co-ordination. The existence of economies of scale in tax collection should not be taken for granted: they will differ from one tax base to another, and indeed may be negative. The influence of the rate of interest on investment in organizational activities was outlined in Chapter 7. The influence of costs depends on the mix and unit cost of each of the specific activities lumped together as co-ordination, relative to the mix and unit cost of each of the specific activities constituting tax collection, other types of administration, and citizen organizational activities. It is impossible to predict, *a priori*, the extent of mismatching that will emerge in the least-cost assignment table. There may in consequence be matching at one jurisdictional level and mismatching at others; some tax-collection economies of scale exploited, and others left unexploited, and some simple bilateral payments and some reciprocal or multilateral networks of financial flows.

An implication of some importance is that if the relative costs of co-ordination are low enough to allow a consequent substantial exhaustion of economies of scale in tax collection, the constituent assembly will assign expenditure functions apparently as if they were independent of revenues. Correspondingly, if the relative costs of co-ordination are high, the constituent assembly will appear to give considerable weight to the availability of tax revenue in the assignment of expenditure functions.

The reader, reflecting on our arguments about mismatching, may find it enlightening to change the focus from the assignment of taxes to the assignment of expenditures. If the cost-minimizing assignment of expenditure functions dictates their decentralization to lower level jurisdictions, and if co-ordination costs and economies of scale in tax collection are such as to dictate their centralization to higher levels, one can interpret the resulting interjurisdictional payments in a new light. Instead of contractual disbursements of revenues, they may now be interpreted as senior government payments for the implementation of expenditure policies (under the decentralized functions) by the lower level governments. It would therefore be misleading to ask whether, in terms of the prior assignment of expenditure functions by the constituent assembly, these payments should be conditional or unconditional. The choice does not arise; all such grants are conditional.[4]

What happens when tax collection does not display either economies or diseconomies of scale? Then, of course, the nature of the co-ordination activities between governments will be different since they will typically involve agreements related to the principle of taxation, whether it should be origin or destination, the type and nature of allowable rebates, and all the issues pertaining to border tax adjustments. Maximizing the yield on this investment will lead the constituent assembly to assign the revenue functions again as if they were independent of the expenditure functions. As in the previous case, the apparent independence will be consequent on the presence of payments that will allow all governments to implement policies under the expenditure powers they have been assigned by the constituent assembly. The flow of funds between governments will again be the outcome of negotiated agreements. Indeed, if the costs of co-ordination were such that a system of payments could not be devised, the constituent assembly would have to assign the expenditure functions in such a way as to guarantee that the governments located at each jurisdictional level could raise enough revenue to implement the expenditure policies they chose.

The necessity of matching powers at each jurisdictional level so that expendi-

---

4 It is worthwhile to define this. To imply that certain payments will always be conditional means only that. It does not limit the breadth of the conditions. Thus conditional grants can be wide, or narrow, in their use; they can demand matching by the recipient, or not; they may or may not be lump-sum, performance-checked, cost plus, regionally or otherwise discriminating, redistributive, temporary, or open-ended.

tures and revenues can be balanced will have an important consequence for the over-all degree of centralization of the public sector. To be specific, where economies of scale in tax collection exist, and where co-ordination costs are high, the constituent assembly must, to economize organizational resources, centralize some or all expenditure functions. It is not unlikely, indeed, that the greater centralization would be achieved by the complete elimination of a lower jurisdictional level.

This conclusion is illuminated if we examine its opposite. Assume therefore that tax collection exhibits diseconomies of scale. The outcome would be the reverse of that discussed above. Unless administration costs were low enough for a senior government to manage several parallel revenue systems, organizational costs would be minimized by decentralization of revenue collection. This would mean that the mismatching would now have the opposite sign to that mentioned above. If co-ordination costs were low enough, agreements could be negotiated to permit taxes collected at the lowest level to be disbursed for spending at higher levels. Thus grants would pass upwards, not downwards. But if co-ordination costs were too high to permit agreed systems of contractual payments (or conditional grants), each level would have to attempt fiscal self-sufficiency. The eventual outcome might be the reverse of that predicted in the last paragraph: expenditures would be more decentralized than if their assignment were independent of revenue assignment, and higher levels of jurisdiction might be eliminated. In other words, diseconomies of scale in tax collection, coupled with high co-ordination costs, could result in a decentralized, Balkanized structure for a public sector.

Turning now to the representative government model, we may continue to use the general framework of the preceding discussion, dropping only the assumption that the constituent assembly minimizes organizational costs. This assumption is now replaced by those used in Chapter 8: that the assignment of all powers is governed by the interaction of politicians, bureaucrats, and citizens in a contest which allows for the existence of degrees of freedom which politicians can dispose of to the benefit of bureaucrats.

Let us therefore imagine any initial, arbitrary assignment table, in which expenditure and taxation powers are mismatched. In such a situation, there will exist some unbalanced budgets out of own revenues, and consequently flows of contractual disbursements within and between jurisdictional levels. The question now arises, would the representative government constituent assembly, inspecting the working of this arbitrarily chosen structure, wish to reassign taxes or expenditure functions, and, implicitly, to change the direction or volume of payments flows?

The answer is already implicit in our analysis of the assignment model of Chapter 8. Bureaucrats will favour the reassignments of tax bases or expenditure functions, if these increase administration or co-ordination activities, or both, while politicians may acquiesce in such reassignment if they have excess degrees of freedom.

In a uni-level assembly, the reassignment process will be dominated by the preferences of the bureaucrats at the jurisdictional level at which the assembly is located; and not by the preferences of bureaucrats at other levels. These bureaucrats will favour centralization of tax bases if the collection of the tax and the disbursements of its revenues entail larger administration and co-ordination outlays than if the occupation of the tax base were decentralized. This tendency will exist even in the presence of economies of scale in tax collection, which the reader should realize work in favour of decentralization because they lead to higher organizational outlays.[5]

In multi-level assemblies, the reassignment process will be complicated by the possibility of conflict between bureaucrats at each jurisdictional level. Because mismatching entails disbursements between governments, it must inevitably give rise to organizational activity concerned with administration and co-ordination at both levels of government. Consequently, although both groups of bureaucrats will favour mismatching of functions and disbursements of revenues, we cannot predict whether that mismatching will be associated with the centralization or decentralization of the public sector.

However, the process described in Chapter 8 as 'trade in functions' suggests that if there are important economies of scale in tax collection, mismatching can result in centralization of tax bases if the savings resulting from the exploitation of these scale economies make it attractive to governments at lower jurisdictional levels to sell, rent, or subdivide (eg, jointly occupy) these bases with the payment financed from the economies realized at the higher level. Thus the payment to the selling level would consist of two parts, one the disbursement of tax revenues, and the other a payment for the power to occupy the traded tax base.[6]

3 GRANTS AS CONTRACTUAL PAYMENTS FOR SPILL-OVERS

Tax collection is but one of the many functions of government in which economies or diseconomies of scale may arise. In this section we attempt to generalize about the conditions under which all such economies and diseconomies, and all negative and positive spill-overs, may entail investment in co-ordination and administrative

---

5 A striking example of this is to be seen in the virtually total centralization of tax bases following the decentralization of some expenditure powers by the Italian government – a typical uni-level assembly – in the early 1970s.
6 See also Section 4 below.

activities, influence assignments, and entail financial payments. Indeed, the general analysis applies regardless of whether the economies or spill-overs stem from private, or public, production and consumption so long as there are interjurisdictional consequences. That part which is concerned with spill-overs has already been discussed in Chapter 4, and our own version set out in Chapter 5.

In this section we wish to show that the mismatching of expenditure and taxation powers and the associated emergence of payments between jurisdictional levels, analysed in the preceding section, was but a special case of a larger class. This larger class contains also spill-overs in consumption, economies of scale in the production of public policies, and any other kind of interdependency that has an interjurisdictional consequence.

It is difficult, both in theory and in practice, to make a clear distinction between the effects of economies of scale and the effects of spill-overs. As between their effects on the behaviour of the residents of adjoining jurisdictions, there may be no distinction. The provision of defence, police, fire, health, education, research, pollution abatement, cultural, and entertainment services in one jurisdiction may be said to spill over into the area of another jurisdiction, there to be enjoyed as external economies. If they are undesirable, they may be termed diseconomies or negative spill-overs. Alternatively, we may consider the costs of provision of such services (or the cost of their prevention): if these show economies of scale, there may be gains to be shared if production takes place in one place instead of two. Such opportunities may lead to more or less formal agreements about the undertaking by one government to make payments in return for the provision or changes in the provision of goods with economies of scale or in the flow of spill-overs. There is a very wide variety of the forms such contractual payments may take. Beneficiaries of services which spill across borders may pay for the benefits they receive or be compensated for the damages they endure. Similarly, a jurisdiction which shares the cost of producing a service may pay for production elsewhere, or be compensated for production which is enjoyed elsewhere.

Normally, therefore, we should expect that the politicians and bureaucrats would enter negotiations concerning such spill-overs, just as (in the previous section) we described negotiations which could lead to the use of taxation powers by one jurisdictional level in return for reimbursement to the other.

However, as between jurisdictions at the same level, the difficulties of coming to satisfactory arrangements may be formidable. We do not in fact observe, in the real world, many such agreements, even when we make allowance for the possibility that the *quid pro quo* may not be in cash, but in the form of some reciprocal service. There are, we may suggest, two reasons for this. First the difficulties involved in two adjoining jurisdictions coming to a workable agreement may be great. One or both parties may look for some other way to remedy the spill-over situation than that to be attained by co-ordination. Second, the difficulties will be compounded when more than two jurisdictions are involved. Additional jurisdictions may now be free riders on the agreements reached by the first two, unless by bargaining some wider agreement may be reached. The costs and difficulties of involving free riders, plus those to implement domestically the policies agreed upon to deal with the spill-overs, may also inspire governments to attempt to avoid the need for co-ordination.

From the politicians' point of view the answer may lie in recourse to a level of government higher than those that are unable to arrive at an agreed contractual payment. For example, in the case of an environmental spill-over, difficulties might be avoided if a higher level of government acted as an agency for the reduction of, or the compensation for, trans-frontier pollution. In this case, funds might flow, indirectly, from one jurisdiction to its neighbour, although they would appear to represent the working of a central government mechanism of pollution, taxation, abatement subsidization, damage compensation, or all of these.

In any case, whether such payments are made between neighbours, or via the intermediation of the central government, their nature will be the same as that already discussed in connection with the disbursement of tax revenues: they will be essentially contractual payments for spill-overs, or for the advantages of services which are produced under conditions of increasing returns to scale.

The reader will readily see that nothing need be added to the discussion of the previous section about the effect of the financing of such spill-overs on the assignment of functions. Under the least-cost model, the burden of co-ordination costs may well lead to the centralization of the provision of such services at a higher level, although the facile assumption that centralization is always indicated if organization costs are to be minimized should be received with scepticism.

Under the representative government assignment model also, nothing new need be suggested. In both the uni-level and the multi-level variants, bureaucrats will welcome the co-ordination outlays that interjurisdictional bargaining and agreement would entail. This suggests, as is indeed the case, that a surprising amount of control over functions that entail spill-overs will be retained at low levels, where the harmonizing of local laws and the negotiation of interjurisdictional agreements provides co-ordination and administrative budgets for local bureaucrats. However, the desire of bureaucrats at senior levels also to be involved in such activities may produce conflict within constitutional assemblies, perhaps only to be resolved by the trading of powers already described.

4 GRANTS AS THE PRICE OF TRADED FUNCTIONS

In Chapter 8, we hypothesized a multi-level constituent assembly in which the *constituants* were politicians, advised by their bureaucrats. Noting that politicians and their attendant bureaucrats at all levels would sometimes want to acquire more functions, and sometimes wish to shed them, we were able to predict the general direction of reassignments by arguing that *constituants* from levels with 'surplus' tax revenues enter an imagined trade in functions as buyers, while those who were short of tax revenues would usually appear as sellers. That is, because a revenue-short government would not be able to acquire a function it desired (unless by coincidence and some permutation of voters in relation to degrees of freedom a revenue-rich government at another level was anxious to shed the same function), while a revenue-rich government would be able to effect a trade, we predicted a drift of powers towards the level with the most productive tax bases. In that chapter we assumed that this drift would, in general, be towards the central level of government.

What would be the outward appearance of such payments? In the case of a purchase they would be payment for a once-for-all transaction, and could take any form: they could be a lump-sum cash transfer; a block grant; the assumption of a local provincial debt; or a payment in kind – that is to say, in the form of a conditional grant, tied to the financing of a policy under some other function. In the case of a loan or of a subdivision, they would be recurrent payments taking the same form as those just described.

We may examine these alternative forms of payment to establish the probabilities of their utilization by *constituants* and bureaucrats. The politicians who are making the payments will not, we would argue, have strong general preferences among them, sometimes preferring one, sometimes another. Their bureaucrats, however, would probably prefer conditional grants to assist expenditures under some function remaining to the selling jurisdictions, for managing conditional grants presents much scope for increases in the administration and co-ordination components of government budgets. The politicians at the receiving end would prefer a form of payment that would increase their degrees of freedom: lump sums, debt transfers, or block grants would all be preferred to conditional grants. Their bureaucrats, like their counterparts at the other level, would have a preference for conditional grants, the co-ordination and administration component of which will be larger, on the average, than those of other forms of payment. However, it is unlikely that provincial and local politicians will be inclined to indulge their bureaucrats' preferences; the very fact that they have been persuaded to rent or sell one of their functions suggests that they are in search of the degrees of freedom and electoral manoeuvrability that comes from discretion in the use of unconditional grants. Thus we would expect that the buying jurisdiction would, because of its bureaucrats' wishes, prefer to pay in the form of conditional grants; while the selling levels' politicians would prefer to be paid in some unconditional form. The former may tend to prevail in routine reassignment of functions, leading to a general multiplication of conditional-grant programs. However, the latter may prevail when new units are being added to a federation, as in the case of Scottish devolution of the 1970s, Newfoundland's joining the Canadian federation in 1949, and Alaska, Hawaii, and other territories joining the United States. In such episodes, we believe, the constitutional settlement has included either assumption of local debt by the central government (the level with the greater revenue powers) or an equivalent arrangement to finance the general treasury of the new jurisdictions.

If the reader doubts the analysis of the latter case – the new state's case – he has but to ask himself: is it likely that politicians at the central level, however well disposed to the new units, would significantly *reduce* their degrees of freedom (their probabilities of re-election) by their choice of the mode of expansion of the government structure? We believe not – they would surely attempt to buy for themselves, in the necessary general settlement following the determination of the new boundaries and assignment of functions, more degrees of freedom, while catering to the local politicians' demand for more revenue without the need to levy new taxes. Both could be achieved by some sort of unconditional financing in return for an expansion of central functions.

In any case, we need not stress that the transaction for which the grant was a payment between the politicians at the two levels may never be popularly known. Thus the grant will be interpreted and explained by the form which it takes, rather than as yet another contractual payment, but this time a part of the assignment process itself, the price of a traded function.[7]

7 The reader will have seen in the last three sections that much of the traditional 'appraisal' and 'evaluation' of conditional grants simply does not fit into our analysis of their role in the assignment process. Thus Scott's own original discussions of the distortions created by conditional grants, in 'The Evaluation of Federal Grants' (*Economica* XIX [November 1952] 377-94), and by all grants, in 'A Note on Grants in Federal Countries' (*Economica* XVII [November 1950] 350-360) do not apply. Neither does Breton's 'A Theory of Government Grants' (*Canadian Journal of Economics and Political Science* [May 1965] 115-81) on the 'optimality' of conditional grants in the provision of certain non-private goods; nor the estimates by James Wilde, 'The Expenditure Effects of Grant-in-Aid Programs' (*National Tax Journal* XXI [September 1968] 340 and 348) and others who have followed his lead in attempting to measure the extent of the incentives created by matching grants; nor the discussions by Lester Thurow, 'The Theory of Grants-in-Aid'

5 GRANTS AS ELEMENTS IN STABILIZING AND REDISTRIBUTIVE
POLICIES

Do the arguments above imply that all grants between governments have the nature of contractual payments, consideration from some implicit transaction? Are there no real transfers? Our answer is that transfers do exist, arising from the stabilization and redistribution functions discussed earlier in Part Three.

We need not devote much space to stabilizing transfers. The reader who turns back to Chapter 11 will see that there are many possible combinations of monetary, fiscal, and exchange rate policies open to governments, and many permutations of the assignment of these among different government levels. Among these permutations and combinations there is scope for payments to be made from the governments responsible for fiscal policy to the governments assigned such functions as public works, transportation, highways, health, regional development, and so on, in general, from taxing or financing jurisdictions to spending jurisdictions. The need for such transfers was first clearly studied in Hansen and Perloff,[8] but many official and academic works since have allocated space to the problem that national governments are not always capable of managing a cyclically variable spending program. Apart from stressing the obvious – that the assignment of fiscal policy responsibilities must take into account the costs of co-ordination entailed by fiscal policy transfers – we have nothing to add to this stabilization literature.

Many systems of federal grants have redistributive formulae: although paid to governments, they take account of population size, age structure, income, indexes of need, and so forth. These characteristics need not be accepted as conclusively demonstrating a redistributive intent, however. It is conceivable that all interjurisdictional payments could be clothed as redistributive transfers, yet actually represent the contractual payments for services or trades discussed in earlier sections of this chapter.

Grants can be arrayed, from the most simple to the more complex, as follows. First there are interperson and interfamily gifts and donations. Voluntary organizations such as the Red Cross and churches both facilitate the collection and payment of such flows and therefore campaign for their increase. Second, there are

(*National Tax Journal* XIX [December 1966] 373-7), by James Maxwell, *Financing State and Local Governments* (Washington: Brookings Institution 1969), or by Wallace E. Oates, *Fiscal Federalism* (New York: Harcourt Brace Jovanovitch 1972) on the alternative forms of conditional grants open to central governments who wish to use them scientifically as instruments to achieve central government objectives.
8 A.H. Hansen and H.S. Perloff, *State and Local Finance in the Natioanl Economy* (New York: W.W. Norton 1944)

flows from governments to recipients in other jurisdictions; pensions, veterans' payments, and compensation for past damages may be the best examples. At the same level are payments from individuals or groups to governments: apart from disaster payments such as those inspired by earthquakes and floods and often administered temporarily by organizations such as the Red Cross, there are few examples of these. Third, there are intergovernmental payments at the same jurisdictional level. These certainly exist internationally, but (again apart from temporary disaster relief) we can think of no examples within a country. Fourth, there are payments from senior governments to governments at lower levels. There are many examples in this category: block grants in the UK, equalization payments in Canada, general tax-sharing in the US, and grants in Australia, not to mention hundreds of payment mechanisms in use between provincial or state governments and their municipalities or school districts, in which income, or need factors, enter into the formulae.

If we ignore, for brevity, the individual and voluntary mechanisms, we must recognize that the grants in the third and fourth categories are not disguised contractual payments, but are all truly redistributive in origin and intent. Our question is, why are there so few in the third category – government to government at the same level – and so many in the fourth – higher-level to lower-level government?

Answers are not obvious. In a way it is a mystery why federal government policies that provide uniform services and transfers across the country and which also promote complementary uniformity of provincially supplied services and transfers are not replaced, or at least complemented, by interregional payments that short circuit the federal treasury. If people in Region R wish government to help people in Region P, why do they turn to their central government, which is necessarily imprecise and averaging in its selectivity, to transmit the desired flows? Why do they not turn to their own government?

Two explanations emerge from our models. First, consider the assignments by a cost-minimizing constituent assembly. A single jurisdiction, at the provincial level, contemplates making transfers to the governments of poorer jurisdictions at the same level, for whom its citizens feel empathy. It must choose which jurisdictions are to receive grants, and how much. Obviously, the organization costs involved can be high. Even its internal administration costs may be daunting, as attempts are made to sort out domestic preferences for 'foreign' recipients. Its co-ordination activities will be even greater as it must negotiate not only with the proposed recipient governments, such as P, but with potential donor governments, such as Q, as well. The cost of the program after all depends on how much other governments like Q are donating, and on how they may be tempted to be free riders.

In our opinion, these co-ordination costs can easily be so great that a cost-minimizing constituent assembly will assign such functions as interjurisdictional redistribution to a higher level. It may, as with the functions discussed earlier in this chapter, be best to regard the central government merely as a clearing house for provincial efforts to help the poorer provinces. If, however, there are economies of scale in the collection of the most productive taxes, then the central government may play a more important role than that of co-ordinator of provincial largesse: it may be assigned the complete responsibility for interprovincial redistribution.

This tentative conclusion is reinforced when we turn to the working of our representative government model. The *constituants* now have personal interests in the outcome. Whatever may be the cost-minimizing mechanism for channelling redistributive payments, the members will have additional preferences which may be expressed in the ultimate assignment. Three pairs of preferences must be considered: politicians and bureaucrats from the central level of government, from provinces such as R and Q which are net donors, and from provinces like P, which are recipients. While it is dangerous to generalize about the interaction of six groups, one conclusion seems to stand out. Of the six groups, only the bureaucrats in the rich provinces have any desire for the intricacy and complication of province-to-province, decentralized, transfer systems. The other five would all seem to be satisfied either with the degrees of freedom or with the increment in budgets gained by a centre-to-recipient system.

We conclude with an example. We feel that in both assignment models the role of the costs of organization activity may be decisive. Our speculations about the outcome of the interaction between politicians and bureaucrats are only that, but they do seem to be confirmed by our observation of international aid and other similar redistributive systems. Viewed through our models, these systems offer donor and recipient countries some choice between multinational and bilateral aid. The bureaucrats of the donor countries prefer the former, but all politicians, and the bureaucrats of the recipients, probably prefer the latter. As well, politicians and bureaucrats in the international organization administering multilateral aid certainly prefer that type of aid. Consideration of the analogues to this example suggest that we need not be surprised that in a federation transfers are centrally administered. After all, in addition to the characteristics of international aid, the central government usually has some discretion over the use of the most productive tax bases.

6 CONCLUSION

The rationale for grants and interjurisdictional transfers in the accepted theory of federalism rests almost exclusively on the desire or need for redistribution. In this chapter, we have sought to show that grants can also play the role of improving the matching of an assignment of revenue and allocation functions based on cost-minimizing or other grounds. Grants are then best conceived as contractual payments. We have also argued that grants can be seen as the price paid by one jurisdictional level for buying or renting one or more powers from another level. And also we have argued that grants can serve to implement the demand of citizens for stabilization. We also recognize the traditional role of grants as serving to implement redistribution.

Index